D1493997

Ruth Robbins is hereby identified as author of this work in accordance with Section 77 of the Copyright, Designs and Patents Act 1988

YORK PRESS
322 Old Brompton Road, London SW5 9JH

PEARSON EDUCATION LIMITED
Edinburgh Gate, Harlow,
Essex CM20 2JE, United Kingdom
Associated companies, branches and representatives throughout the world

First published 2001

ISBN 0-582-43149-2

Designed by Vicki Pacey
Phototypeset by Gem Graphics, Trenance, Mawgan Porth, Cornwall
Colour reproduction and film output by Spectrum Colour
Produced by Addison Wesley Longman China Limited, Hong Kong

C ONTENTS

PART ONE

INTRODUCTION

HOW TO STUDY A NOVEL

Studying a novel on your own requires self-discipline and a carefully thought-out work plan in order to be effective.

- You will need to read the novel more than once. Start reading it quickly for pleasure, then read it slowly and thoroughly.

- On your second reading make detailed notes on the plot, characters and themes of the novel. Further readings will generate new ideas and help you to memorise the details of the story.

- Some of the characters will develop as the plot unfolds. How do your responses to them change during the course of the novel?

- Think about how the novel is narrated. From whose point of view are events described?

- A novel may or may not present events chronologically: the time scheme may be a key to its structure and organisation.

- What part do the settings play in the novel?

- Are words, images or incidents repeated so as to give the work a pattern? Do such patterns help you to understand the novel's themes?

- Identify what styles of language are used in the novel.

- What is the effect of the novel's ending? Is the action completed and closed, or left incomplete and open?

- Does the novel present a moral and just world?

- Cite exact sources for all quotations, whether from the text itself or from critical commentaries. Wherever possible, find your own examples from the novel to back up your opinions.

- Always express your ideas in your own words.

This York Note offers an introduction to the reading of *Villette* and cannot substitute for close reading of the text and the study of secondary sources.

Charlotte Brontë's last novel is not a text that gives up its pleasures easily. In contrast to *Jane Eyre*'s energetic heroine and fast-paced romantic plot, *Villette*'s heroine, Lucy Snowe, is elusive and shadowy, living a slow, mundane life. Yet it does reward the reader's patience with a much more complex and rounded picture of human life, and of female life in particular, than was usual in Victorian fiction. In a famous essay by Charlotte Brontë's near-contemporary and fellow woman novelist George Eliot, the writer castigates the common view of life in fiction by women. The essay 'Silly Novels by Lady Novelists' (1856) **parodies** that era's staple diet of **romantic fiction** – the novels written by and for women:

> The heroine is usually an heiress, probably a peeress in her own right, with perhaps a vicious baronet, an amiable duke, and an irresistible younger son of a marquis as lovers in the foreground, a clergyman and a poet sighing for her in the middle distance, and crowd of undefined adorers dimly indicated beyond. Her eyes and wit are both dazzling; her nose and her morals are alike free from any tendency to irregularity; she has a superb *contralto* and a superb intellect; she is perfectly well-dressed and perfectly religious; she dances like a sylph, and reads the Bible in the original tongues.

The typical heroine has every social advantage – she is a peeress; she is adored by many men; and she is beautiful and intelligent. How different, Eliot implies, from the homely lives of most readers of these novels.

Lucy Snowe, by contrast, has none of these advantages. She is not a peeress or an heiress. She might be intelligent but she is not adored. She is moral, but she is not pretty. Her clothes are blameless but not exciting; we never see her dance; and she quite definitely reads the Bible in English. Whatever could Charlotte Brontë have been thinking of to have such a dull heroine?

A clue comes perhaps from George Eliot's satire on feminine fiction (op. cit.). Eliot clearly implies that the usual depiction of romance is inadequate because it is unrealistic. The fictional characters share nothing with the everyday world of their readers, and the fantasy is dangerously seductive because of its unreality. Charlotte, aware of her own physical imperfections (she was small, plain, short-sighted), wanted to write books that reflected lives like her own – the lives of ordinary women. She told her sisters that Jane Eyre was 'as plain and as small as myself to demonstrate that a heroine could be interesting even if she was neither beautiful nor privileged. She wanted to give significance to the kinds of life that are generally left out of fiction. This impetus also informs *Villette*, where Lucy's concerns about her appearance, and her attempts to rise above such petty considerations, make up much of the psychological story within the novel. Lucy is sometimes far from admirable, but she is living a life with real difficulties to overcome.

This is not to say that the whole novel is unremittingly **realistic**. There are many touches of the **Gothic** and the supernatural around the edges. These, though, always have natural explanations, and they supplement the psychological story of Lucy's life. The questions that *Villette* asks are: How can a woman live in a society that does not value her properly? What life can a woman have if she does not fit into the usual romantic stories of courtship, marriage and motherhood? Lucy's story answers these questions: 'with difficulty'. This is not a romance or a **fantasy** but a story about the real. As such, it has its pains – but it also has its rewards.

PART TWO

SUMMARIES & COMMENTARIES

The text referred to in this Note is the 1985 Penguin Classics edition of *Villette*, edited by Mark Lilly and introduced by Tony Tanner. As it contains detailed notes, which are particularly helpful in explaining the French language in the novel, this Note does not include translations.

SYNOPSIS

Villette is the story of Lucy Snowe, a young woman orphaned early. The first chapters of the novel deal with her visit, aged about fourteen, to Mrs Bretton, her godmother. At Bretton, she observes her godmother's son, Graham Bretton, and a child who comes to visit, Polly Home.

As a young woman, Lucy finds a post as a paid companion to an elderly invalid, Miss Marchmont. When Miss Marchmont dies, Lucy journeys to Villette, a town in Belgium. She arrives unannounced at Madame Beck's school and is taken in to work as a nursery governess to the headmistress's children before becoming an English teacher.

Life at the school is arduous and Lucy is lonely. She is half in love with the school's English physician, Dr John, and she has a bantering relationship with one of the older English pupils, the flirtatious, shallow Ginevra Fanshawe. On being left alone in the school during the holidays, Lucy suffers mental collapse. She is rescued by Dr John and his mother (in fact the Brettons) now living in Villette, and they renew their friendship. Lucy continues to work at the school, where she waits with feverish anxiety for signs of interest from Dr John. He, however, is in love with the worthless Ginevra. His hopeless infatuation is eventually resolved by the accidental meeting and renewal of ties with Polly Home and her father. By the end of the novel, Dr John has fallen in love with Polly and married her, Ginevra having eloped with a penniless aristocrat, Alfred de Hamal. (Ginevra and Alfred are responsible for a subplot that plays a large part in Lucy's mental state. They cover their meetings in the

school by drawing on stories that the buildings are haunted by a nun;
Alfred disguises himself in a habit and 'haunts' Lucy.)

Meanwhile, Lucy is increasingly attracting the notice of Paul
Emmanuel, a master at the school and a cousin of Madame Beck. He
singles Lucy out for his unconventional attention, and several small
episodes over many months attest to the growing affection between them.
Madame Beck and her family are horrified by this, and plot to separate
the two of them for both religious and family reasons.

Monsieur Paul, as he is known, resists Madame Beck's
machinations. He delays his departure to be sure of seeing Lucy before
he goes abroad on family business. He has arranged a future for her – a
small school of her own. His intention is to marry her on his return from
the West Indies. The ending of the novel, however, is **ambiguous**, and it
is left to the reader to imagine one of two alternatives: either M. Paul
returns to marry Lucy, or he is shipwrecked on his return journey, leaving
her to face life alone.

VOLUME 1

CHAPTER 1   Life at Bretton

The narrator is enjoying the calm at her godmother's house. Mrs Bretton,
a good-looking, middle-aged widow, has one son, Graham, a handsome
and lively boy.

An old acquaintance asks Mrs Bretton to take care of his daughter,
Polly, while he travels for his health. She is a tiny, doll-like child, aged
six, and is distraught about her father's departure. Polly shares a bedroom
with the narrator, but does not settle easily. Mrs Bretton hopes that she
will become calmer when she finds someone in the house to feel affection
for.

> One of the strange features of this **autobiographical fiction** is the
> elusiveness of the narrator. In this first chapter, her life is made
> mysterious, not illuminated. We are given none of the usual
> information – her age, her parentage, her social standing; even her
> name is withheld from the reader. Just the vaguest hints are
> dropped about her background, but no concrete information is
> forthcoming, a feature that the narrative will repeat many times.

Lucy is, however, a close observer of other people's lives. The details of Polly's movements and attitudes are thoroughly narrated, deflecting attention from the narrator. Polly is presented as tiny and fragile: 'she looked a mere doll; her neck, delicate as wax, her head of silky curls' (p. 64). One of the things that Lucy insistently notices is that although Polly looks doll-like, she has a mind and will of her own – there is a mismatch between her fragile appearance and strength of mind. The **disjunction** between appearance and reality will be a central theme.

the sojourn of Christian and Hopeful reference to the spiritual journey of two characters in John Bunyan's *Pilgrim's Progress* (1678–84)
more than one of whom wrote *de* before his name a sign in French of aristocratic lineage

CHAPTER 2   **Polly's father visits; Graham Bretton comes home and meets the little girl**

At first Polly does not settle. Her behaviour is good, but Lucy describes her as 'haunting' the house. A change comes over her, though, when her father comes to visit.

At the same time, Mrs Bretton's son Graham also returns to the house. He immediately makes Polly's acquaintance with exaggerated formality and insists that he will become her favourite. Only when Polly announces her own bed-time does Graham treat her as a child, lifting her up against her will. With great indignation, she leaves the room, demanding to know what he would do and feel if she were to pick *him* up like that?

The intensity of Polly's homesickness, and then of her feeling for her father, feel to Lucy like unnatural sentiment: 'I, Lucy Snowe, plead guiltless of that curse, an overheated imagination; but whenever, opening a room-door, I found [Polly] seated in a corner alone, her head in her pigmy hand, that room seemed to me not inhabited, but haunted' (p. 69). This is an important statement, since it is the first time that Lucy has named herself. Furthermore, she describes herself negatively, saying not what she is, but what she is not. In seeing Polly as a figure of the **uncanny** (she is like an animated doll who appears to be 'haunting' the house), Lucy suggests that her own imagination is 'overheated', despite her earlier denial that it is any such thing.

Polly changes when Graham arrives, **foreshadowing** subsequent events in the novel when the two will meet again as adults. The **parody** of adult conversation that he conducts with her is both funny and natural: it is ordinary for a teenaged boy to tease a little girl, and for her to take that teasing more seriously than he does. There will be important differences when they do meet again.

irid Charlotte Brontë's idiosyncratic term for 'iris'
nonpareil without equal; a paragon
chemisette bodice or apron

CHAPTER 3   **Polly and Graham's friendship grows**

When Mr Home leaves Bretton, Polly is inconsolable, but eventually she begins to accept Graham as a substitute. Polly is only interesting and animated in Graham's company. Her attitude to him is one of devoted service. The reward for her devotion is romping and tumbling, but also attention and talk, which she values more. They quarrel only once, on Graham's birthday, when he has a tea party for some of his schoolfriends from which Polly is excluded. She is devastated. For a few days she will not forgive him, and though she does come round, Lucy notes that Polly is more reserved with Graham.

The visit lasts for two months before Mr Home sends for Polly. The little girl is shaken by the news: she will be glad to see her father, but is sad that she will lose Graham.

That night, when Lucy goes to bed in the room she shares with Polly, the child is overwrought. Lucy carries her to say goodnight to Graham in the hope that it will calm her, and then delivers a sermon about not expecting or demanding too much love from her playmate. As she watches the child depart the next morning, she speculates about Polly's future, wondering how her sensitivity will survive the knocks of ordinary life.

One of Brontë's themes is unrequited, unequal love. The relationship between Polly and Graham – a girl of six and a young man of sixteen – makes interesting watching for Lucy. Graham's relative indifference and Polly's slavish devotion are, Lucy sees, dangerous to the little girl. She is exposed by her emotional need and will have to learn to repress her emotions if she is to survive in the real world. This is a recurrent theme in Brontë's writing. Lucy learns this lesson by watching Polly rather than through loving and being loved herself. Moreover, although the inequality between Polly and Graham is presented as natural and ordinary, we are supposed also to read it as an **analogy** for the relative positions of the sexes in the adult world at that time, where men are considerably more powerful than women. Polly's tiny, doll-like stature serves a double function in the narrative: it is both a realistic portrayal of a little girl and a symbolic representation of the powerlessness and infantilism of **femininity** in wider society.

Why hast thou forsaken me? an approximation of Christ's last words on the cross, hence an expression of extreme agony (Matthew 27:46)
the Grand Turk sultan of the Ottoman Empire, who required perfect submission and service
Odalisque female slave in a harem
Candace dynastic name of the queens of Ancient Ethiopia
Mount Blanck ... Kim – kim – borazo Mont Blanc is the highest mountain in western Europe; Kimborazo is the highest mountain in South America

CHAPTER 4   **Lucy's career as a nurse-companion**

Lucy leaves Bretton shortly after Polly's departure. She asks us to picture her happy and contented for the next eight years; after that time she was thrown upon her own resources. She resumes her narrative with the story of her career as a nurse-companion to the wealthy Miss Marchmont, an elderly, slightly forbidding lady crippled with rheumatism. Despite Miss Marchmont's occasional fits of temper, Lucy is patient and tolerates the very limited life her post permits. One night, Miss Marchmont is woken by a storm; in a moment of intimacy, she tells Lucy the story of her lost lover, thrown from his horse and killed before they could marry, thirty years before. The story seems to soothe the old lady, but in the morning she is dead.

This relatively brief chapter is very significant for our understanding of Lucy's character and narrative mode. Again, she tells her story indirectly, refusing to give us straightforward information about her life and feelings since leaving Bretton.

> It will be conjectured that I was of course glad to return to the bosom of my kindred. Well! the amiable conjecture does no harm, and may therefore be safely left uncontradicted. Far from saying nay, indeed, I will permit the reader to picture me, for the next eight years, as a bark slumbering through halcyon weather, in a harbour still as glass. (p. 95)

This is a devious narrative method which is repeated often through the novel. Lucy offers us a version of her life that we are permitted to imagine, but undercuts the 'amiable conjecture' by pointing out its imaginary status.

The chapter is also important for introducing the question of how unmarried middle-class women are to earn their living. Lucy cannot undertake manual work, the traditional province of working-class women, because it would lead to a loss of her own class status. The roles of governess and paid companion are the only respectable occupations open to her. These occupations, however, were poorly paid and had no prospects.

These facts are not merely a sociological commentary on the lot of poor middle-class women in Victorian England. They also allow Lucy to comment in detail on her own particular character and its formation: she is 'Tame and still by habit, disciplined by destiny' (p. 97). What she has gained from the experience of working as a paid companion is self-control and discipline.

Finally, this chapter is important because it **foreshadows** later events. The figure of the woman waiting in vain for her lover is a repeated image in Victorian literature (see, for example, Tennyson's 'Mariana' [1830] or Charles Dickens's Miss Havisham in *Great Expectations* [1860–1]). Miss Marchmont's tragic love story might seem rather out of place in this novel. Yet its significance is that it predicts the position in which Lucy will find herself at the end of her story.

halcyon calm and carefree
the legend of the Banshee in Irish myth, a 'woman-fairy' alleged to wail when
death is coming to a house

CHAPTER 5   Lucy goes to London

Miss Marchmont's death leaves Lucy without a job or a home. She
decides to go to London and look for further opportunities.

Seeking one's fortune in London is a traditional plot line, but it is
far more usual for a male protagonist to take this route than for a
female one. Lucy's feelings of fear and confusion, her uncertainties
about where to go, and her difficulties in commanding the respect
of the inn's servants are all related to the fact that she is a lone
female in an anomalous position. A lady should not, at this period,
be travelling alone; Lucy's unchaperoned existence leaves her
painfully exposed. The will to undertake this journey marks her out
as determined and unusual.

Another interesting feature is Lucy's self-description. She says of
herself: 'I had a staid manner of my own which ere now had been
as good to me as a cloak and hood of hodden gray' (p. 104). This is
one of relatively few statements that Lucy makes about herself and
her demeanour – and it is typically a statement about disguise rather
than revelation.

Babylon city of Ancient Mesopotamia associated with luxury and decadence.
In literature London has often been called a modern Babylon

CHAPTER 6   Lucy leaves for the Continent. On the sea journey she
meets Ginevra Fanshawe

The following morning, Lucy decides to go abroad. She takes a berth
on a ship bound for the Continent and spends the journey in observation
and judgement of the other passengers. One young lady, Ginevra
Fanshawe, is returning to school in Villette, the capital of Labassecour,
and strikes up a conversation with Lucy. The young lady is no scholar,
and her expensive education, paid for by her godfather, appears to
have been wasted. Her goal is to marry a rich man and she pities
Lucy for having to earn her own living. Lucy feels strangely happy

and calm, despite her precarious position, and is sad when her journey is over.

One of the key ways that we learn about Lucy is through the statements and judgements she makes about others rather than through direct statements she makes about herself. Her views of her fellow passengers are important not so much for what they say about those people, but for what they tell us about Lucy's standards of judgement. She comments on their demeanour, physique and dress, and she speaks of her horror that a young, pretty woman might be the wife of a vulgar, short, fat man. From the point of view of plot, however, the most significant event is Lucy's first meeting with Ginevra Fanshawe. Although we do not know it yet, Ginevra will be important in Lucy's life and they will eventually establish a strange rapport.

The description of the sea voyage and the feeling of calm it engenders in Lucy is a significant repetition of an already-established motif of the novel. In her non-description of her life after leaving Bretton (Chapter 4, p. 94), Lucy used the **metaphors** of a sea journey and a shipwreck to describe how she had been living. Now the metaphor is **literalised**. Lucy's life is 'all at sea': she has no firm ground such as might be provided by a family or wealth; she has no anchor to hold her in conventional modes of behaviour. In this chapter she experiences her journey as both a time of freedom and a suspension of the need to act and make decisions. Thus arrival on firm ground is not the pleasure one might expect. For Lucy, arrival means that she must act on her own behalf and face an uncertain future. The confusions over language and money she suffers on disembarking indicate the difficulties of the path she has chosen.

Jonah's gourd in the Old Testament (Jonah 4:5–6), Jonah needed shelter from the harsh sun. God caused a gourd to grow miraculously quickly to give him shade

Boue-Marine fictional place name, meaning literally 'sea mud'

the Styx and of Charon ... in Egyptian and Greek mythology, the river Styx separates the lands of the living and the dead; Charon is the boatman who rows dead souls across the water for a small fee

quakerism a non-conformist religious grouping; its members were noted for plainness in dress

jeunes Miss young ladies – a French phrase for designating English girls

inconvenant both inconvenient and unconventional

surveillance supervision

blasée indifferent about a pleasure because one has experienced it too often

steerage passengers those travelling in the cheapest accommodation

Schönes Mädchen beautiful girls

chose thing or 'thingy'

Villette ... Labassecour literally 'little town' and 'the low court', Brontë's names for Brussels and Belgium respectively

As poor as Job Job was deprived by Satan of all his worldly possessions. Shakespeare uses the phrase 'as poor as Job' in *Henry IV, Part 2*, I:ii

half-pay a salary paid to army and navy officers after retirement, or when no longer in service

Stone walls do not a prison make ... from the poem 'To Althea from Prison' by Richard Lovelace (1618–58)

CHAPTER 7   **Lucy arrives in Villette without her luggage. She becomes lost and frightened, but eventually acquires employment and shelter at Madame Beck's boarding-school**

The next morning Lucy goes to Villette, prompted by Ginevra who had said that her headmistress wants an English governess. When she arrives, she discovers that her trunk has not been loaded on to the coach, so she is destitute. She appeals for help to a fellow English passenger, who discovers that her trunk has been left at Boue-Marine and will be forwarded. The English passenger gives her the address of a suitable inn, and accompanies her for part of the way. When he leaves her alone, Lucy becomes lost after being pursued by a couple of men on the street.

While trying to find her way, she finds herself outside Ginevra's school. Lucy decides to try her luck. The headmistress, Madame Beck, is persuaded to take a chance on the new arrival only by the intervention of her cousin, M. Paul. At Madame Beck's request, he studies Lucy's face and concludes that it will be safe to give her a job.

This is a chapter based on two coincidences – one of which is clearly displayed, the other withheld until a later point in the story. From Ginevra's chance words, Lucy decides to go to Villette; from the unlucky chance of getting lost, she amazingly finds herself at the door of the very house she is seeking. In addition, as we will discover much later, the English passenger who helped Lucy with her lost luggage and directed her to an inn is none other than Graham Bretton. Her withholding of information, as we have already seen, is a consistent trait.

Diligence stagecoach

the speech of Albion English: Albion is a poetic name for England

physiognomy ... Read that countenance the idea of being able to deduce moral character from facial features (the pseudo-science of physiognomy) was very popular in Victorian times. M. Paul is being asked to make a judgement about the honesty or otherwise of Lucy's face

CHAPTER 8   Lucy, now the nursery governess at Madame Beck's, learns about her mistress and is promoted to the role of English teacher

Lucy is conducted through the school (once a convent) to her bedroom, which she will share with Madame Beck's children. In the dead of night she is woken by the noise of Madame Beck rifling through her new employee's belongings. While Lucy feigns sleep, the headmistress also takes impressions of the keys to her trunk, desk and workbox so that she can examine their contents when they arrive.

Madame Beck is a handsome but stern woman, with little warmth. She is charitable, but harsh where she finds fault, and runs her school with a rod of iron. She maintains discipline by 'surveillance' – constant spying.

Lucy's job as a nurse soon comes to an end when Madame Beck asks her to teach English to the girls of the second class. Lucy is apprehensive, knowing that she will have to maintain discipline with limited French. There is a battle of wills between teacher and pupils, which Lucy wins. Madame Beck, who has been watching through the keyhole, is impressed.

Madame Beck is one of the central figures of the novel. She serves both as a foil to Lucy (whose opposite she is in many ways) and as a point of comparison. For example, Madame Beck 'had no heart to be touched' (p. 137), while Lucy, on the other hand, is a passionate woman. They are similar, however, in their watchfulness: Lucy lives through observing other people's lives, while Madame Beck uses observation as a management tool. Although there is something very creepy about Madame Beck (she literally creeps about her own house in silent shoes), Lucy is torn between disgust and respect for her, perhaps because she recognises in her mistress something of her own manner. Watching – or its near synonyms, spying, gazing, looking – is established as a major theme. Madame Beck is a supremely competent watcher, and would be undetected by anyone other than Lucy, who watches just as obsessively. And here is a source of discomfort for the reader. Lucy is supposed to be our heroine – the emotional and sympathetic centre of the novel – but when her watchfulness borders on **voyeurism**, the reader becomes complicit in an activity of which we disapprove.

Anglicé or Hibernicé in English, or in Irish-English

un véritable Cachmire a genuine cashmere – therefore of very great value

Aurora Roman Goddess of the dawn

bourgeoise usually translated as middle class; but bourgeois(e) is not just a statement of social standing – it also means attitudes that conform strictly to contemporary notions of propriety

Minos one of the three judges of hell in Greek mythology; Madame Beck is a firm judge against whom there is no appeal

Ignacia a feminine form of Ignatius, and thus an allusion to Ignatius Loyola (1491–1556), founder of the Jesuits, a Catholic order of priests. Throughout the novel the author is highly critical of many aspects of Catholicism, so calling Madame Beck Ignacia is a back-handed compliment

Not the agony in Gethsemane, not the death on Calvary the Garden of Gethsemane is where Christ spent a night of mental torment in anticipation of his coming crucifixion on Calvary

hornbook a first book for children, its cover being made of horn

tell it not in Gath a proverb meaning, 'don't let your enemies know'. Gath was supposed to have been the birthplace of the Old Testament giant, Goliath (II Samuel 1:20)
jeune fille literally 'young girl'; Lucy is distinguishing between the poets' ideal of the maiden and what young women are actually like

CHAPTER 9   Lucy learns more of the Labasscourienne girls, and tells us more about Ginevra

Lucy pronounces her new life as a teacher arduous but satisfying. She finds the Labasscourienne girls devious and lazy, with little self-respect compared to English girls. Despite this, she manages to make herself liked, and satisfies Madame Beck. In only one area is she regarded with suspicion – her Protestant religion – and steps are taken to ensure that her influence will not infect the school.

Lucy reintroduces Ginevra, whom she had met again on taking up her employment. Ginevra is shallow, vain and insubstantial, but Lucy likes her. Ginevra makes Lucy her confidante and tells her of an admirer she has nicknamed Isidore. This relationship is, on Ginevra's side, heartless. She enjoys the attention, but feels only mild contempt for him. Lucy remonstrates with her, but Ginevra is unrepentant.

On one occasion, Ginevra is wearing a splendid set of jewels, which Lucy suspects are a gift from the secret admirer. She tries to make Ginevra understand that such gifts should come only from openly accepted lovers, but Ginevra is incorrigible: she has already begun a flirtation with another man. Her only wish is to enjoy her youth, and she does not care who she hurts in the process.

The relationship between Ginevra and Lucy is an odd one to say the least. They are absolute opposites, yet, despite temperamental differences, the two get on. Ginevra may not like being preached at by Lucy and usually resists her sound advice, but at least with Lucy she is able to be herself and stop acting the part of glamorous **femininity** demanded by her social world. As she says to Lucy, with reference to the mysterious Isidore:

He thinks I am perfect: furnished with all sorts of sterling qualities and solid virtues, such as I never had, nor intend to have ... I am far more at my ease with

CHAPTER 9 continued

you, old lady – you, you dear crosspatch – who take me at my lowest, and know
me to be coquettish, and ignorant, and flirting, and fickle, and silly, and selfish,
and all the other sweet things you and I have agreed to be a part of my character.
(p. 155)

Indeed, it may well be that Lucy is the only person who sees
Ginevra as she really is.

Ginevra's function in the novel is like that of Polly Home in the
earlier chapters. Lucy learns about the expected roles of women in
society in her observations of both girls, although they provide a
very stark contrast to each other. Polly thinks of femininity as
entirely bound up with *giving* love and duty to others; Ginevra
thinks of her femininity in terms of *receiving* admiration and
presents. One of the things that Lucy searches for is an alternative
vision of femininity that permits self-respect rather than the self-
abasement of either service or coquettishness.

Diogenes Greek philosopher renowned for austere living and straight talking

CHAPTER 10   **After one of Madame Beck's children has an**
accident, a new doctor comes to the school

Even with her children, Madame Beck is never tender. One day, when
her daughter Fifine breaks her arm, Madame Beck leaves the child in
Lucy's charge while she goes for a surgeon. On her return with an
unknown doctor, it is Madame who calmly aids him, despite the child's
terrible pain. The doctor is impressed with her, and Madame is taken
with the handsome stranger. As he departs, Lucy realises that he is the
stranger who helped her when she first arrived in Villette.

The handsome English physician, Dr John, visits regularly to tend
to Fifine's broken limb. Lucy discerns a kind of flirtation between him
and the headmistress, and when he notices her staring at him, demands
to know what there is of interest in his face. Lucy stays silent.

The glimpse offered by this chapter into the home life of Madame
Beck is instructive. We have been told that she always behaves
properly, but also that she has no heart, no emotions, no tenderness.
For the Victorian reader, the fact that this coldness applies even to
her relationships with her children would have been profoundly

shocking. Motherhood was upheld as the highest role for women in mid-nineteenth-century culture; it was revered as an ideal state. In that sexually repressed era, the only love a woman was permitted to voice openly was that for her children. Nineteenth-century readers would certainly have regarded Madame Beck as monstrous because of her apparent lack of maternal instinct.

CHAPTER 11 **Madame Beck seems attracted to Dr John, but the doctor himself appears to have another lady in mind**

That summer Dr John continues to be a regular visitor at the school, giving rise to gossip and parental concern. But Madame rides the storm and soothes the parents.

One day, Lucy overhears Dr John pleading with someone in the portresse's cabinet. When he leaves the room, he is clearly in some distress. Lucy wonders what is going on. She returns to the sickroom, where Madame Beck and the doctor are with the little girl.

When he leaves a few moments later, Madame Beck, who had been animated in his presence, seems exhausted. She looks tired and old as she gazes into a mirror. She later abandons her fancy for the doctor, deciding that it is ridiculous and against her interest.

A common figure of ridicule in literature is that of the older woman in love with the much younger man. Madame Beck, in her infatuation for Dr John, takes all kinds of risks. She risks her business and the wrath of scandalised parents, and she risks her dignity by becoming the target of gossip among her staff and servants. This chapter shows Madame Beck both running these risks and overcoming them. Her professionalism deals with the slander on the reputation of her school, while her self-command deals with the realisation that she is simply too old to fall in love with Dr John.

The chapter also establishes a mystery. With whom is Dr John pleading in the portresse's cabinet? This is one of very few occasions when Lucy does not simultaneously know the answer to the question she asks.

a large organ of philoprogenitiveness phrenology, the study of skull shape
and size, purported to find links between bumps on the head and moral
virtues and vices. The Labasscouriens have large bumps that apparently
show they love their children

Apollyon the devil in John Bunyan's *Pilgrim's Progress*; he has a massive
physical contest with the hero, Christian, which is an allegory for a struggle
of conscience

CHAPTER 12   Lucy discovers a casket containing a love letter and
bouquet of violets addressed to someone in the
school. Dr John is anxious to get the casket back, but
he is not its sender, and Lucy does not know who it
was intended for

The school and its garden are said to be haunted by a nun. Lucy dismisses
the story and enjoys the garden for its solitude and silence. One evening,
while seated in a secluded spot, she is disturbed when an object thrown
from one of the overlooking windows lands at her feet. It is a casket
containing a bunch of violets and an anonymous love letter 'For the grey
dress'. She wonders for whom it is intended, and is about to go indoors
when Dr John enters the garden. He wants to recover the casket,
although he was not its sender. He is distressed by the letter and asks
Lucy what she will do with it. But before they can settle any course of
action, Madame Beck appears in the distance and the doctor disappears.
Lucy meets her mistress openly, but knows that Madame's suspicions
have been aroused.

This chapter works in several ways. First, it is important for
imparting a vaguely **Gothic** air to the novel through the story of the
ghostly nun, an atmosphere of the supernatural which will be
important for Lucy's responses to later actions in the plot. Second,
it furthers the plot by setting up questions that will be answered
only later: to whom is the casket addressed, who is it from, and
what does Dr John have to do with it?

Most importantly, though, it reveals a little more of Lucy's
character to the reader. Her predilection for solitary walks
reinforces our impression of her as an unsociable being who values

privacy and silence over community and chat. But we also discover that although Lucy usually *acts* as if she is content with her lot and grateful for her new life, she is in fact disguising turbulent emotions. In the garden she thinks of her secret longings for 'something to fetch me out of my present existence, and lead me upwards and onwards' (p. 176). But she also speaks – in a very telling and violent **analogy** – of her exercising an iron will to repress desires she cannot fulfil. She uses the biblical story of Jael and Sisera, an horrific murder in which an army captain (Sisera) is killed by Jael hammering a nail into his skull while he is sleeping, to describe what she does to her unruly desires: she knocks them on the head, she says, a **cliché** that gains real force through the image of the murder. It is a phenomenal effort of self-control.

Methuselah the oldest man in the Bible; he is described as living to 969 years old in Genesis 5:27

salut the evening service

Jael to Sisera in the Old Testament (Judges 4:1–24) Sisera was an army captain who presided over a brutal regime until he was killed by Jael. She drove a nail into his skull while he was sleeping

Heber Jael's husband

CHAPTER 13 **Madame Beck spies on Lucy and listens in to her conversation with Dr John to try to discover why she had met him in the garden**

One evening Lucy goes to the dormitories and discovers Madame Beck going through her belongings. Lucy does not betray her presence, and slips silently away to the classrooms instead.

Little Georgette is recovering from a fever, but Madame Beck notices that she still has a slight temperature, and decides to call for Dr John, leaving Lucy to receive him. Lucy recognises a plot. When the doctor arrives, Lucy hears the portresse cross-question him about the casket. Apparently, he had been attending a little boy in the neighbouring school, and had seen the casket dropped from the window. It had nothing to do with him personally. Lucy later sees another missive being thrown from the same window. She fetches the letter and shows it to Dr John. He tears it up without reading it. Before he can tell Lucy who the letters are for, there is the sound of a sneeze at the door. Madame Beck, who has been spying on them, has given herself away. She comes calmly into the room, and Lucy leaves her alone with the doctor.

In a highly significant passage in this chapter, the reader receives more information about Madame Beck's processes of surveillance. The moment her suspicions are aroused by Lucy and Dr John, she goes through Lucy's things. Lucy watches this invasion of her privacy with 'secret glee' and admiration for Madame's neatness. 'Had I been a gentleman,' she writes, 'I believe madame would have found favour in my eyes' (p. 186). Lucy knows, however, that she must be not be caught in this observation; if Madame were to discover her, the consequences would be disastrous:

> ... there would have been nothing for it but a scene, and she and I would have had to come all at once, with a sudden clash, to a thorough knowledge of each other: down would have gone conventionalities, away – swept disguises, and *I* should have looked into her eyes, and *she* into mine – we should have known that we could work together no more, and parted in this life for ever. (p. 186)

Eye contact is generally taken as a sign of frankness and honesty. Madame Beck's relationship with Lucy is conducted through sidelong glances, which convey distrust. That attitude, however, is mutual: if Madame Beck is sneakily looking into Lucy's life, Lucy is sneakily looking into hers.

Madame finds nothing untoward among Lucy's belongings. At first the fruitless search amuses Lucy: it is funny that so much effort will yield nothing. Later, though, she finds herself distressed and cannot explain why. She is not upset because Madame distrusts her: 'I did not care twopence for her mistrust' (p. 187). It is for the reader to surmise that Lucy is upset because it exposes how small her life is: she has no secrets – no lovers, no letters, nothing for Madame Beck to discover. Lucy wants to be loved, but where is love to come from in a life like hers?

stories like that of Conrad and Elizabeth of Hungary Elizabeth, Queen of Hungary (1207–31), devoted her life to a very severe regime of poverty and self-denial; Conrad was her spiritual adviser

Mause Headrigg ... Sergeant Bothwell characters in Sir Walter Scott's novel *Old Mortality* (1816)

Meribah's waters Meribah is the site where Moses struck a desert rock and water flowed out (Exodus 22:7)

Light-heart the Beggar proverbial saying meaning that a beggar might as well laugh since he has nothing to lose

CHAPTER 14   **On Madame's birthday, Lucy acts in the school play; she also discovers Isidore's identity**

Madame Beck's birthday is a school holiday marked by a feast, a play directed by M. Paul, and a dance. Lucy hides away from all the bustle, but is discovered by M. Paul, who demands that she take part in the play as one of the girls has dropped out. Lucy agrees reluctantly, and he locks her into the attic to rehearse. Eventually, he returns, hears her part and tells her she must appear in male costume. Lucy refuses the costume she is offered, and adapts it herself so that she wears only part of the male attire.

Nervous as she is, Lucy plays her part well; she is a fop competing for the attentions of a coquette played by Ginevra. As she watches the vain young girl's performance, she realises that Dr John is in love with Ginevra. At the ball that evening, Lucy resorts to her familiar role of observer. In the middle of the evening, Ginevra takes Lucy to the dressing-room and confesses that she is over-excited because both her admirers are present. She offers to point them out: Count Alfred de Hamal is a delicate dandy; Isidore, it turns out, is Dr John. Returning to the house from the garden, Lucy meets the doctor and tells him that she knows of his love, and she hints that Ginevra is worthless. He will not be persuaded, and they go their separate ways.

How are we supposed to judge the worth of the people we meet? This question exercises Lucy in this chapter, but she is also forced to consider how others judge her. The fête is a day of celebration, when everyone makes an effort with their appearance, but Lucy does not wish to draw attention to herself since she knows that others will judge her negatively. However, her performance in the play makes her the centre of attention, and her feelings about this are quite painful: 'A keen relish for dramatic expression had revealed itself as part of my nature; to cherish and exercise this new-found faculty might gift me with a world of delight, but it would not do for a mere looker-on at life.' She forces herself to repress the idea of pleasure in self-display, and retires during the ball 'to a quiet nook, whence unobserved I could observe' (p. 211), a phrase that sums up her whole life. When forced to look at herself closely by Ginevra as they stand side by side in front of a large mirror, Lucy can be philosophical – can judge Ginevra as pretty, but can also see her faults. In her conversation with Dr John at the end of the chapter, however, she is brought up short by his blindness over Ginevra, whom he judges entirely by appearance, saying:

> She is so lovely, one cannot but be loving towards her. You – every woman older than herself, must feel for such a simple, innocent, girlish fairy, a sort of motherly or elder-sisterly fondness. Graceful angel! Does not your heart yearn towards her when she pours into your ear her pure, child-like confidences? (pp. 221–2)

When Lucy, in a spirit of **irony**, makes the same point about the handsome looks of Alfred de Hamal, Dr John cannot see the irony at all. Their conversation points out sexual inequality. De Hamal is good-looking, says Lucy; he is not manly, says Dr John. Ginevra is beautiful, says Dr John – and he can admit of no other criteria for judging a woman. Thus the theme of appearance and reality, and its connection to gender, is amplified here.

bénitier holy-water basin
moyens ways, habits
amour-propre literally self-love, but used to designate self-respect

CHAPTER 15   Lucy is left alone and becomes depressed and ill. After attending confession at a nearby Catholic church, she collapses and loses consciousness

When the examinations and prize-givings are over, the school closes for the long vacation. Lucy remains with only a few servants and a retarded girl, abandoned by her family. When even the girl is taken on holiday, Lucy is alone.

One evening, in deep distress, she goes to a Catholic church and asks the priest for solace. The priest is surprised by this Protestant girl, and he sends her away so that he think over her case, asking her to meet him the following day. Lucy has no intention of keeping such an appointment, fearing a conversion attempt. When she leaves the church, however, she collapses in the porch of a nearby building and loses consciousness.

At several points in the novel so far there have been hints that the calm manner Lucy maintains is a fragile veneer. She has many of the symptoms that we would now attribute to depression. Its causes have to do with the fact that her life, though safe, is very limited and confined; moreover, she has no positive outlet for emotions such as love and tenderness. This is a very anti-Catholic novel, and Lucy, in her usual state of mind, regards Catholicism as a religion demanding unthinking obedience to unreasonable dogma; it is, therefore, a mark of her desperation that she should seek any kind of comfort in a Catholic church.

Babylonish furnace in the Old Testament Book of Daniel, Daniel and his companions are placed in a furnace, but they do not burn
Rue des Mages literally Magi Street. The Magi were three wise men from the East who visited the infant Christ in the stable; the word 'magi' also implies wizardry
Fénélon François de Salignac de la Mothe Fénélon (1651–1715), a Catholic priest and writer associated with relatively liberal and undogmatic views

VOLUME 2

CHAPTER 16   Lucy regains consciousness

Lucy comes round in surroundings that are strangely familiar to her. She seems to be at Bretton with her godmother, though Mrs Bretton does not recognise her. When Graham returns from work, Lucy greets him as Dr John, and discloses to the reader that she had recognised him long since, though neither he nor his mother have yet recognised her.

That evening Mrs Bretton realises that her guest is Lucy Snowe, her goddaughter. They spend the rest of the evening catching up on the stories of their lives since they last met.

Lucy recognises Dr John many pages before she meets him at his mother's house, but refuses to share her knowledge with the reader. Why? Her own stated reason is: 'I had preferred to keep the matter to myself. I liked entering his presence covered with a cloud he had not seen through, while he stood before me under a ray of special illumination' (p. 248). There is a perverse pleasure in recognising someone when he does not recognise her, and in Lucy's dull life, such secrets add a certain spice. There is also pain, however, at not being recognised. It confirms that Lucy is – what she will later be called by Dr John – 'an inoffensive shadow'. There is nothing about her that makes her special in other people's eyes.

CHAPTER 17 **Lucy continues to recover. She discovers how she was brought to the Brettons' house and is diagnosed as suffering from hypochondria**

The following evening, Dr John discusses Lucy's illness with her. He diagnoses it as hypochondria, which he cannot treat because it comes from her mind. He also tells Lucy how she came to be at Bretton. He had been returning from a house call when he came upon a priest he knew attempting to lift the unconscious Lucy. The priest had been worried about the woman who had come in strange circumstances to his confessional; he had decided to follow her home to make sure she got there safely, but she had fainted. Lucy explains that what had driven her to the church was loneliness and depression, not a crisis of faith. She is anxious that Père Silas (the priest) should not find out where she lives, for he might try to convert her.

> Two key issues arise here. The first is the diagnosis of Lucy's illness as hypochondria, a complaint of the mind that comes from unhappy circumstances and a limited life. The second point of interest is that Lucy does not expect other people to understand how she feels – especially not robust, cheerful people like her godmother and Dr John. Her mental distress will not bring sympathy from most observers. The nineteenth century was not generally sympathetic to mental illness. Indeed, one contemporary critic (for the *Spectator*) described Lucy as having a 'morbid sensibility', accusing her of being responsible for her own sufferings, as though she should just

'snap out of it'. One of the remarkable things about this novel is that it does attempt to explain a depressed mental state in a character in whom contemporary readers would have discerned a weakness or sin rather than an illness.

the waiting waters will stir in John 4:4, the pool of Bethesda was a still sheet of water. At certain times an angel would descend from heaven and stir the water; the first person to bathe in the pool thereafter would be cured of his ailments

Azrael the Angel of Death in the Islamic tradition

Hypochondria morbid (unwholesome) sensibility or depression, rather than feigned or psychosomatic illness

Benjamin's portion the largest share. In the Old Testament (Genesis 43:34), Joseph held a banquet for his brothers, and the youngest of them got the largest portion

CHAPTER 18   **Dr John and Lucy discuss Ginevra**

Lucy continues to stay with the Brettons, waiting for Dr John to broach the subject of his love for Ginevra. At last he does so, singing her praises and lamenting his own lot as the unfavoured lover. When Lucy can stand it no more, she tells Dr John that his infatuation makes him slavish, and he is offended. She apologises later and the two are friends again. He now even begins to seek her out to discuss his love; indeed, he is so vehement that he almost persuades Lucy that Ginevra is indeed the paragon of virtue that he believes her to be.

> Throughout the novel, Lucy has been an observer and judge of other people's actions. In this chapter she is almost brought to suspend her judgement of Ginevra's shallow, selfish nature. With Ginevra no longer before her eyes, and only the version of her produced by Dr John, she has nothing on which to form her views. This is very much a novel based on seeing: and when one cannot see, one cannot judge or know the world.

CHAPTER 19   **Lucy meets M. Paul at the art gallery**

Although term has recommenced, Lucy stays at La Terrasse, the Brettons' home, a little longer with Madame Beck's permission. Her stay passes pleasantly, with lots of excursions to the galleries of Villette. One day, while contemplating a painting of Cleopatra – a picture of which she strongly disapproves – she is encountered by M. Paul. He is shocked that Lucy is unchaperoned, and leads her away from the semi-nude Cleopatra to what he deems a more suitable group of pictures of female piety. Lucy, however, refuses to accept his right to direct what she is permitted to look at, dismisses his choice of pictures as hideous and asks him to move out of the way so that she can observe the crowds. Among the new entrants to the gallery she sees Alfred de Hamal, and she watches him as he looks at the Cleopatra, simpering over it and clearly amused. A little later Dr John enters the room; he too sees the painting, though it is certainly not to his taste. Lucy watches and compares the two men before she is escorted from the gallery.

> In Chapter 14, Lucy and Dr John had had an argument about the rights and wrongs of judging women and men by their appearance. In this chapter, that theme reappears. First of all, there is the appearance of Madame Beck at the Brettons' home. In public, Madame is full of life and dignity; in private, as she leaves in her carriage, Lucy sees that this is merely a **masquerade**, a performance that cannot be maintained. She is impressed by what Madame achieves through acting, but knows that appearances do not always reflect reality.
>
> In this chapter, which offers several idealised versions of **femininity** from the paintings in the gallery – the magnificently sensuous Cleopatra, the virgin, the bride, the mother and the widow – Lucy demonstrates her resistance to simplistic judgements of femininity. The Cleopatra might be unconventional (she's only half-clothed, for example), but the demure ladies in the other four pictures are worse because they are hypocritical images. These are pictures of women always in relation to men. Even the maiden is lying in wait for her mate. They have no existence in their own right, and Lucy rejects them as role models and as works of art.
>
> She gets her own back on masculine values when she observes the male viewers in the gallery and judges them by their appearance. Alfred de Hamal is described in terms that make him sound foppish and effeminate; Dr John is more manly and handsome. But she

does not judge *only* by appearance. She also looks at their responses to the pictures. De Hamal's attitude to the Cleopatra is giggling and silly. Lucy's description of him calls into question not only his manliness but his maturity. Dr John, on the other hand, is dismissive of the painting, and Lucy approves his much more grown-up reaction. Most interesting of all is what M. Paul says of the picture. He tells Lucy that the woman in the painting has a magnificent figure, but she is in no way a woman one would marry, or whom one would wish for a sister or daughter. In other words, he can appreciate an image of sensuality, but he regards respectability and propriety as the key virtues of femininity. These two virtues, however, depend on behaving conventionally. They leave no space for the woman to think for herself, so Lucy rejects his aesthetic and moral judgements.

Earlier in the chapter, Lucy has commented explicitly on the difficulty of distinguishing someone's real character merely by looking at them when she remarks that there are two contradictory views of Dr John – the public man and the private citizen – and the two views do not match (p. 273). This is an implicit reference to what came to be known as the **separate spheres debate**, a controversy that raged in the mid-nineteenth century about the relative positions of men and women. Men were supposed to belong primarily to the public sphere of action, women to the private sphere of domesticity. But men, of course, had access to both spheres; they had paid employment outside the home, but they also lived in domesticity. Thus, Lucy suggests, men have two selves – one they display in the world outside, one they keep for the fireside. Women, by contrast, were not supposed to be so complex – hence the habit of judging them by appearances. But, as we have already seen with Madame Beck, the woman who works is anomalous in this scheme of things: she, like a man, has a public and a private life, and is therefore more complex than first appearances might suggest. The same can also be said of Lucy.

Père la Chaise the most famous cemetery in Paris
Nebuchadnezzar's hottest furnace in the Old Testament (Daniel 3), Daniel and his companions are consigned to roast in a furnace by King

Nebuchadnezzar, but they miraculously survive – thus bringing about the
king's conversion

fruit of the Hesperides the golden apples of Greek mythology

sheltie Shetland pony, noted for being very small

le type du voluptueux the epitome of sensuousness

mulatto person of mixed racial descent – certainly intended here as a term
of abuse

CHAPTER 20   **Lucy and the Brettons go to a concert and Dr John
falls out of love with Ginevra**

Still with the Brettons, Lucy is invited to a concert. Mrs Bretton insists
that she have a new dress for the occasion, which she chooses: it is pink,
and Lucy is mortified. They enter the concert hall together and observe
the crowds, teasing each other, though Lucy is momentarily upset by
seeing her own image in a mirror. Meanwhile, the musicians take their
places, shepherded there by M. Josef Emmanuel and his half-brother, M.
Paul. There is a moment's hush while the royal party enters its box. In
the royal train are lots of young girls, one of whom is Ginevra. Dr John
later sees Ginevra sneering at his mother and the insult cures him of his
infatuation.

When Dr John and Lucy return to their seats after the interval,
Lucy realises that M. Paul is looking with disapproval at her new dress.
She does not meet his glance. Although the doctor is now free of his love
for Ginevra, he continues to talk about her; he tells Lucy that he fears
something more serious than flirtation is going on between Ginevra and
Alfred de Hamal. Lucy dismisses his view.

This chapter resumes the novel's obsession with looking. The
concert itself is less important than the opportunity it offers Lucy
for observing the social world of Villette. On the other hand, while
she may look at others, they too can look at her. This is
compounded by the fact that, for once, Lucy is dressed in a way
that excites attention – her new pink dress. Indeed, she catches
sight of herself in a mirror, not at first realising that it is herself,
and is brought up short by her own disappointing appearance:
'Thus for the first, and perhaps only time in my life, I enjoyed the
"giftie" of seeing myself as others see me. No need to dwell on the

result. It brought a jar of discord, a pang of regret; it was not flattering' (p. 286).

The most significant event of the chapter is Dr John's realisation that Ginevra is not an angel after all. Her attitude to his mother dispels his illusions.

giftie gift; allusion to Robert Burns's poem 'To a Louse': 'O wad some Pow'r the giftie gie us / To see oursels as others see us!'
Jacob or Esau in the Old Testament (Genesis 23), both Jacob and Esau (sons of Isaac) left home to search for wives
Rhadamanthus in Greek mythology, one of the three judges of hell, and thus a byword for harsh justice

CHAPTER 21   **Lucy returns to school with a promise from Dr John that he will write**

At last Lucy has to go back to school. Dr John promises to write so that she will not feel forgotten. Alone in the dormitory, Lucy gives herself a severe talking to. The promise of Dr John's letters has made her foolishly happy, but she feels there is no point in being so excited. In the refectory, she is accosted by M. Paul, who realises that she is sad. He questions her, teases her a little, and even says one or two almost tender things until he makes her cry and she demands to be left alone.

A fortnight later Lucy receives her first letter, which she locks away in the dormitory to read later, savouring the anticipation. In her classroom, meanwhile, M. Paul has reduced half the class to tears, and now turns his harangue on Lucy, who also weeps. He realises he has gone too far and offers Lucy his handkerchief. As he leaves, he asks Lucy about her letter. He tells her to bring back the handkerchief when she has read the letter: he will be able to tell if it is from a lover or a friend by the look in her eyes. Later, however, when Lucy is alone, idly tossing and catching the handkerchief, M. Paul creeps up on her, accuses her of laughing at him and snatches the handkerchief away.

M. Paul certainly takes an interest in Lucy. When he accosts her in the refectory, he has been watching her and has read her mind. Later in the chapter, when he shouts at her and her class, it seems as if he has been provoked by her not returning his interest, and by her having a life that has nothing to do with him. These are hints to which the careful reader should pay attention.

This chapter also contains a lot of Lucy's internal life and opinions. Of special interest is her self-control – her will to stop herself living in fantasies and to make herself face the reality of her situation. On the one hand, then, Lucy clearly feels attracted to Dr John; on the other, she knows that he is merely being kind to his mother's goddaughter. **Repression** of unwarranted feelings, Lucy believes, is the only way for her to live: she asks her Reason: 'if I feel, must I *never* express?' and receives the answer: '*Never!*' (p. 307). Love and desire are not for her.

We also discover here Lucy's views about learning and literature. She reads primarily for pleasure, and her views are very instructive in relation to the novel in which she appears. She writes:

I dearly like to think my own thoughts; I had great pleasure in reading a few books, but not many: preferring always those in whose style and sentiment the writer's individual nature was plainly stamped; flagging inevitably over characterless books, however clever and meritorious. (p. 313)

What is significant here is the emphasis on Lucy's own individuality (she likes to 'think her own thoughts') and on her unconventional taste in literature. In the world of the pensionnat, where the watchwords are *convenance* (convention) and *décence* (decency), unconventionality is never approved. Indeed, it is probably true to say that conventionality is regarded as one of the key virtues of mid-nineteenth-century femininity. Lucy's rejection of convention sets her apart.

Nebo the mountain from which Moses saw the Promised Land that he was destined not to enter (Deuteronomy 34:1–5)

Timon the melancholic and misanthropic hero in Shakespeare's play *Timon of Athens*

bas-bleu bluestocking, a term used since the eighteenth century to describe intellectual women

Cyclop's-eye of vermilion red in Greek mythology, the Cyclops is a one-eyed monster who is blinded when Odysseus pokes him in the eye with a sharp stick; here it refers to the dabs of red sealing wax on Lucy's letter

CHAPTER 22   **Lucy reads her letter in the school attic and is disturbed by a ghostly apparition**

That evening, in desperation to find some privacy to read her letter, Lucy takes it to the attic. The letter gives her a few moments of intense pleasure, but she is disturbed by what seems to be the ghostly figure of a nun. In a panic, she rushes to Madame Beck's sitting room and demands that everyone there should go and investigate. They all accompany Lucy back to the attic, but no one is there and her letter has gone. More upset now by the loss than by the apparition, Lucy becomes frantic until she is calmed by Dr John himself – one of Madame's guests whom Lucy had not spotted. He leads her gently from the room, then restores the letter to her: he had picked it up on entering the attic.

The doctor gets Lucy to describe what she has seen. He tells her that it was a 'spectral illusion'. The only cure for such manifestations is to 'cultivate happiness' (p. 330). This angers Lucy; she does not believe that happiness can be managed in that way, but she is worried about her own state of mind. The searchers in the attic had found nothing unusual. Lucy never uses the word 'nun' to anyone but Dr John. Eventually the subject just drops away.

The apparent sighting of a ghost in the attic is one of the key moments in establishing a **Gothic** atmosphere in this novel; such a ghost is a **stock character** of Gothic fiction. But more than that, it is significant for what it does to the reader's perception of Lucy's character. We already know that she is occasionally an unreliable narrator, who deliberately withholds important information. On this occasion, however, we do not know whether she has actually seen something or not. We know that she is overwrought, so perhaps Dr John is correct to suggest that the apparition is a product of her troubled mind. Even Lucy herself recognises that the reader might come to such a conclusion: 'Say what you will, reader – tell me I was nervous or mad; affirm that I was unsettled by the excitement of that letter; declare that I dreamed: this I vow – I saw there – in that room – on that night – an image like – a NUN' (p. 325). The very syntax of her declaration – its repeated dashes, its breathlessness and its compromised certainty (an 'image like a nun'

: continued

_ .1ot exactly a nun) – suggests that the rational explanation of nervous over-excitement could be true.

CHAPTER 23   **Lucy accompanies Dr John to the theatre to see the actress Vashti. When a fire breaks out, the doctor rescues a girl from the ensuing crush**

In the weeks after the nun episode, Lucy receives regular letters from Dr John. Her first replies, full of warmth and feeling, are never sent; she writes them merely for her own relief. What the doctor actually receives are brief, reasonable letters. One evening, he turns up unannounced to take her to the theatre to see the performance of a great actress. Lucy unthinkingly goes to get her chosen outfit from the attic. At the far end of the dark room there appears to be a light, but the moment she arrives it is extinguished; she fetches her dress, rather shaken, and returns downstairs. Dr John immediately suspects that she has seen the nun again. Lucy denies it, but is not believed.

At the theatre Lucy is initially impressed by Vashti's performance, but later is almost terrified by its power. The actress is neither morally good nor conventionally beautiful, but she is a brilliant performer. She wonders what Dr John thinks, and realises that he is entirely unmoved by Vashti's performance. Suddenly, there is a cry of 'Fire!' and panic sets in among the audience. Lucy and Dr John see a girl being trampled beneath the feet of the crowd and the doctor sets off to rescue her. They and the girl's father escape together. The girl has an injured shoulder, so Dr John and Lucy accompany the father and daughter back to their apartments to tender their aid.

> In Chapter 19 Lucy claimed that Dr John has two personalities – a public persona and a private one (p. 273) – and we noted that, as a man, he is allowed to indulge both personalities. In the early part of this chapter, we see that Lucy also has at least two selves: a public, rational self governed entirely by repression and self-control, and a private self that is based on feeling rather than reason. The two sets of letters she writes to Dr John (one of which is never sent) demonstrate her complexity. Interestingly, she is also keen to insist to the reader that she is not hopelessly in love with the doctor. In an aside, she writes:

I disclaim, with the utmost scorn, every sneaking suspicion of what are called 'warmer feelings': women do not entertain these 'warmer feelings' where, from the commencement ... they have never once been cheated of the conviction that to do so would be to commit a mortal absurdity: nobody ever launches into Love unless he has seen or dreamed the rising of Hope's star over Love's troubled waters. (p. 335)

Lucy is protesting too much. Her reason might tell her that Dr John is not going to fall in love with her, but that hardly means she does not feel those 'warmer' feelings.

This chapter also reprises the theme of images of women in its description of Vashti. Lucy is very ambivalent about this public spectacle. She sees much to admire in it, but also recognises that the actress has paid a terrible price for her performance. Her two opposing comments – 'It was a marvellous sight: a mighty revelation. It was a spectacle low, horrible, immoral' (p. 339) – speak again of the complexity of human beings, of the impossibility of judging simply by appearances. Dr John's response is more conventional: 'he judged her as a woman, not an artist: it was a branding judgment' (p. 342). The point here is that Lucy is involved in trying out different possibilities for female existence, hence her fascination with watching the different types of women around her. Vashti is not a role model she will follow, but that does not prevent her from seeing something marvellous in her acting genius. Dr John, who represents more conventional views of the world, judges the actress differently. For him, her talent is unimportant. The essential features of a woman reside in her appearance and her morality: Vashti is ugly and immoral, therefore Vashti is worthless. He regards convention and decency as absolutes; Lucy sees them as stifling constraints, so she is able to admire even what disturbs her.

Hebe Greek goddess of youth and cup-bearer to the gods. She had the power of restoring youth and beauty to the old

Rimmon a Syrian god whose shrine was at Damascus. To bow down to a god other than the Christian deity, Lucy is suggesting, is a kind of idolatry

a day of Sirius a dog day, when the weather is very warm. Sirius is the name of the Dog Star

neat-handed Phillis a country maiden in Milton's poem 'L'Allegro'
Vashti in the first chapter of the Old Testament Book of Esther, the great
beauty Queen Vashti refuses to appear before her husband, King Ahausu-
erus, and his court. As a result the king made a proclamation that all wives
must obey their husbands
Saladin sultan of Egypt and Syria (1138–93), and adversary of Richard I
during the crusades
Paul Peter Rubens actually Peter Paul Rubens (1577–1640), Flemish
painter renowned especially for his fleshly nudes
Tophet a place of horror in the Old Testament (II Kings 23:10 and Isaiah
30:33)
Pythian reference to the Greek myth about faithful friends: when Pythias is
sentenced to death by a tyrant, he is allowed to return home to sort out his
affairs, leaving his friend Damon as security. To the tyrant's surprise,
Pythias does return, and the strength of the two men's friendship prompts
him to release them both

CHAPTER 24   After some weeks of neglect, Lucy is invited to La
Terrasse, where she meets the girl who was crushed
at the theatre

For seven weeks after Vashti's performance, Lucy hears nothing from the
Brettons. She finally gets news of them from Ginevra, who complains
bitterly to her about the boring evening she has just spent with her
godfather, M. de Bassompierre. It turns out that he is the father of the
girl injured at the theatre, and Mrs Bretton and Dr John were also present
that evening as guests.

The next morning Lucy goes through what has become a routine
torture: awaiting letters in the knowledge that she will be disappointed.
On this occasion, however, there is a letter – from Mrs Bretton rather
than her son. It invites Lucy to La Terrasse that evening.

On arrival at the Brettons', Lucy meets Miss de Bassompierre and
is astonished to discover that she already knows the seventeen-year-old
girl before her: she is Polly Home from the old days at Bretton.

When Lucy had first known little Polly, she had seen her as a fairy-
child, an **uncanny**, doll-like creature. Those feelings recur at La
Terrasse: 'Before the glass, appeared something dressing itself – an

airy, fairy thing – small, slight, white – a winter spirit' (p. 378). Lucy, in trying to analyse Polly's unearthly quality, concludes that it is not her appearance (though she is certainly pretty), but something that comes from inside her – a spirit, a light, that makes her different from ordinary pretty girls. Lucy never quite puts her finger on it, but Polly seems to have a moral quality that other girls are lacking.

Barmecide's loaf imaginary nourishment. In the stories of *The Arabian Nights*, a beggar is invited to the home of a rich merchant, Barmecide, and given empty dishes. The beggar humours his host's joke, and is eventually given good food to eat

Esculapius in Greek mythology, the doctor who attended the Greek armies during the Trojan war; in later myths, he became a kind of god of medicine

Nebuchadnezzar ... his baffled Chaldeans in the Old Testament Book of Daniel 4:7, King Nebuchadnezzar has a dream that his soothsayers (the Chaldeans) are unable to interpret

CHAPTER 25   **When snow makes a return to school impossible, Lucy has a further opportunity for observing Polly the next day**

When Dr John and M. de Bassompierre arrive home that evening, they go to the kitchen to warm themselves, and Lucy watches the happy family scenes between father and daughter, son and mother. During the evening tea, the doctor's eyes are often on Polly. He is fascinated.

The following morning, Lucy notes that Polly is not always childish and gay; she has another set of manners that are ladylike and quiet. These are most evident with adults other than her father.

This chapter is taken up with Lucy's observations of Polly Home. Although she does not draw explicit conclusions from what she sees, it is clear that Polly is more complex than she at first appears. With her father, she behaves like a child: teasing, playing games, worrying over him, expending all her energy on his comfort. But she later shows that she is capable of greater maturity. Lucy remarks on a change not just of behaviour, but even of appearance when Polly's father is absent:

... all the child left her; with us, more nearly her companions in age, she rose at once to the little lady: her very face seemed to alter; that play of feature, and candour of look, which, when she spoke to her father, made it quite dimpled and round, yielded to an aspect more thoughtful, and lines distincter and less *mobile*. (p. 371)

In other words, Polly is different people for different audiences: her character is a series of sophisticated performances, each made to suit those she is with.

Old Christmas Father Christmas
dreadnought overcoat
pas de fée, ou de fantaisie fairy dance or fantasy

CHAPTER 26   Lucy buries her letters and encounters the nun again.
              Her friendship with Polly continues

From now on, Lucy has plenty of variety in her life. Madame Beck approves of her new acquaintances, and gives her leave to go out whenever she wants. The headmistress is more trusting because she broke into Lucy's workbox and read Dr John's letters. But Lucy is shocked later to discover that the letters have been tampered with again – this time, she guesses, by M. Paul. The intrusion into her privacy makes her take extreme measures to hide the letters safely. She is burying them beneath the old pear tree when her attention is attracted by a moving shadow, and she is approached by what appears to be a veiled woman. The two of them stare at each other for a few moments before Lucy demands to know what the apparition wants; when she approaches, the figure disappears.

Meanwhile, Polly has become fond of Lucy and invites her to be her paid companion. Lucy refuses this offer. Repeating a German poem about love one evening, Polly says to Lucy that loving is less important than being loved. She has been upset by her cousin Ginevra boasting that Dr John is in love with her, and that she could marry him at any moment. Lucy proposes that Ginevra's powers be put to the test. The following day there is to be a gathering at the Hôtel Crécy of men of science, including Dr John. Lucy is to bring Ginevra so that Polly can see whether he loves her or not.

A number of themes come together in this chapter and interlock in quite surprising ways. Lucy's letters are scrutinised by Madame Beck, but they pass the test of discretion, so Lucy will no longer be spied on by Madame.

But as Madame Beck's surveillance wanes, M. Paul's interest seems to grow. Lucy is prompted to bury her letters because she suspects that he has read them. Then, in burying the letters – burying her own happiness – Lucy again comes across the nun. Her first encounter with this figure was also associated with reading Dr John's letter (Chapter 22), and the second encounter occurred as she was preparing to go out for the evening with him (Chapter 23). Relinquishing the letters seems to call up the apparition again. This association is significant: it implies that the feelings – whether happy or melancholy – that the letters cause provoke the nun's appearances.

Finally, Lucy explicitly concludes what the previous chapter was hinting: that Polly's personality is a series of performances tailored to the audience she is with: 'She had different moods for different people' (p. 384). Of the moods she describes, the two important ones are Polly's behaviour towards her father, where she continues to play the child, and Polly's behaviour towards Dr John: 'With Graham she was shy, at present very shy; at moments she tried to be cold; on occasion she endeavoured to shun him' (p. 384). Her shyness and coldness provoke a rebuke from her father, but he sees her too much as a little girl to guess the reasons for it. He would find it hard to believe that she is old enough to be in love.

Sinbad   in the stories of *The Arabian Nights*, Sinbad the sailor discovered a valley filled with diamonds

Ichabod   a figurative way of saying 'regret'. Ichabod was a child born after the death of his father in the Old Testament (Samuel 4:19–21)

blue   as in bluestocking – an intellectual woman

Undine   a water nymph

'Des Mädchens Klage'   'The Maiden's Lament' by the German poet Johann Schiller (1759–1805). The lines quoted translate thus: 'Oh, thou Holy One,

call back your child; / I have enjoyed all earthly pleasures, / I have lived and
I have loved'

CHAPTER 27   An evening of learned conversation is held at the
Hôtel Crécy, where Lucy is the subject of one of
M. Paul's outbursts

Lucy and Ginevra visit the boys' college in Villette for a lecture by one of
the professors. Lucy is both surprised and amused to discover that the
speaker is M. Paul, but is impressed by his speech. When it is over and
her party are leaving, Lucy is approached by M. Paul and asked what she
thought of it. She cannot answer adequately, being too shy. The professor
is invited to join the party at the Hôtel Crécy later that evening.

At dinner Lucy observes Polly and Ginevra. While Ginevra is the
more obviously pretty of the two, Polly has subtler attractions. Although
the gentlemen at the meal are all aged men of science, Polly is able to talk
sensibly to them – something that Ginevra cannot do. Ginevra perks up
only when Dr John arrives and is seated beside her. But her conversation
is not at the right pitch for the occasion. Later, in the drawing room, she
is dull and flat until the gentlemen rejoin them. Dr John joins Lucy so
that he can watch the two girls at his ease. Suddenly M. Paul comes
across and whispers savage judgements of Lucy in her ear. Dr John hears
and realises that the professor is jealous of his conversation with Lucy. He
stays laughing and teasing Lucy to annoy M. Paul until the crowd around
Polly clears and he joins her.

As Lucy awaits the carriage, M. Paul begs forgiveness for insulting
her, which Lucy conditionally gives. Ginevra, who has not enjoyed the
evening and is furious with Dr John's indifference to her, rails against him
and everything else until Lucy loses patience and rebukes her soundly.

After the months where nothing happened to Lucy, there is now a
whirl of social engagements and new scenes for her to observe. Here
we see her continue to watch over Polly and Ginevra, and to
compare and contrast the merits of the two girls. Her judgement,
though muted, is decidedly in favour of Polly. This is also the
beginning of the romance between Dr John and Polly. He too has
amended his judgement of Ginevra, saying she is 'certainly a fine
girl', the handsomest girl in the room (p. 401), but his thoughts are

elsewhere. He tries to disguise his interest in the adult Polly by talking about her when she was a child – neither Lucy nor the reader is fooled. His alacrity in joining her, and his shyness with her, are clear signs that he is falling in love.

In addition, whatever there is between Lucy and M. Paul is also speeding up. Why, one might ask, among an audience of important people, would the professor seek out Lucy's opinion on his speech? And why, when he sees her in conversation with Dr John, is he jealous enough to come and whisper insults at her? Of course, he is right to discern that Lucy is partly in love with the doctor. This chapter contains her nearest admission of this fact. Where before she had declared that a woman never falls in love where she knows there is no hope (Chapter 23), here there are definite hints that her feelings for Dr John are warmer than she has previously suggested. She regrets that 'while Graham could devote to others the most grave and earnest, the manliest interest, he had no more than light raillery for Lucy, the friend of lang syne' (p. 401). Presumably 'manly' interest implies desire. And when he calls her 'a being as inoffensive as a shadow':

> I smiled, but I also hushed a groan. Oh! – ... These epithets – these attributes I put from me. His 'quiet Lucy Snowe', his 'inoffensive shadow', I gave him back; not with scorn, but with extreme weariness; theirs was the coldness and the pressure of lead. (p. 403)

Dr John has no capacity for seeing her as a woman who is capable of being loved. M. Paul, on the other hand, is presumably expressing his own rather strange interest in her through his jealous outburst.

bonne maid
gros-bonnets large hats – 'bigheads'
Nero Roman emperor (AD 15–68), famous mainly for acts of extreme cruelty
soubrette a flirt, but also a go-between in romantic comedy
Mon ami, je vous pardonne My friend, I forgive you. The point at issue here is that the French word *ami* means both 'friend' and 'beloved'; Lucy resists the latter meaning when she insists on speaking the word 'friend' in English

a John Knox to a Mary Stuart John Knox (1513–72) was the key Protestant
adversary to Mary, Queen of Scots (1542–87). He published a vitriolic
attack on both Elizabeth I and Mary as female rulers, entitled *First Blast of
the Trumpet against the Monstrous Regiment of Women* (1558)

VOLUME 3

CHAPTER 28   Lucy interrupts M. Paul's lesson and breaks his glasses. That evening he lectures her on ostentation and social pretension

M. Paul cannot stand his lessons to be interrupted. One morning, Lucy
is sitting in the corridor listening to his increasing fury at a series of
interruptions, when she is asked to deliver a message. Although the
professor has threatened to hang the next intruder, Lucy creeps into the
room and approaches him at his desk. When he demands a cord and
gibbet to hang her with, she furnishes him with her embroidery thread.
She delivers the message that he must go at once to the boys' college but
he refuses. To persuade him, Lucy picks up his mortarboard in readiness
for his departure, but she accidentally drops it, breaking his glasses in the
process. Lucy is dismayed and afraid, but M. Paul is gentle and departs
meekly.

That evening he makes one of his impromptu visits to the school to
read to the girls during the study hour. Lucy is working on something
intended as a gift. M. Paul decides to sit next to her, but when she moves
to make space for him, he misunderstands and takes offence. He then
rearranges the room, with Lucy seated as far away as possible. Later that
evening, he lectures her, saying that she has the most difficult character
of any woman he has ever met, and is too concerned with outward
appearances and her social life. He has also noticed that her clothes have
recently become fashionable and showy. Despite this harangue, they part
on good terms. That night Lucy muses on his lecture and seems almost
pleased by it.

One of the things that is often missed in this text is its humour.
Lucy's approach to M. Paul's desk, after he has expressly forbidden
any more interruptions and threatened to kill the next intruder, is

one such moment. The production of embroidery silk for a noose – with its manifest unfitness for the purpose – is amusing. Similarly, M. Paul's lecture to the plain, modest teacher about her worldly manners and ostentatious clothing is clearly at odds with what she is really like. Shared humour is typically a symptom of love, so the fact that Lucy does not take offence at the offensive things M. Paul says suggests a growing mutual regard.

une petite casse-tout a little daredevil. *Casse-tout* is particularly apt here because it literally means 'one who breaks everything' as well as 'one who dares anything'

at Jericho a long way off. In the Old Testament (II Samuel 10:5), when King David's soldiers had their beards shaved off, they were told to stay at Jericho until they had grown again

CHAPTER 29   **Presents are given to M. Paul for his birthday by everyone but Lucy**

The following morning Lucy gets up early to finish off the watchguard she is making for M. Paul's birthday. When he arrives, the school gathers to present him with flowers. When he has received all the bouquets, he appears still to be waiting for something – only Lucy has produced no present. His exaggerated disappointment makes her decide to keep her present a little longer. M. Paul launches into a lecture to the assembled school. At first Lucy does not listen, but eventually she realises that M. Paul is lambasting the English nation, and its women in particular. He promises the girls that he will take them on a day out when the spring comes. Lucy, however, declares that she will not go, since she does seem to be his friend.

That afternoon Lucy goes to her classroom to get the watchguard from her desk. There she finds M. Paul rifling through her belongings. She knows he often opens her desk, corrects her studies, lends her books and leaves her sweets, but she has never before caught him in the act. He asks why he received no present from her hands, so Lucy offers it now. M. Paul is absurdly happy and they part friends. When he returns to the school that evening during study hour, he seeks Lucy out and spends the evening with her.

Lucy is a devious narrator who deliberately withholds information from the reader in different parts of the novel. This chapter is full of knowledge that is deliberately deferred. First, there is the simple fact of whose are the 'certain initials' carved on the gift-box: who is the watchguard intended for? That question is answered quite quickly, but why does Lucy refuse to tell us straight out? Moreover, we discover only now that she has been in the habit of receiving gifts of books and sweets from M. Paul. Why has she not told us before? Two kinds of answer come to mind. First, we know that Lucy is very aware that she is unattractive to men. She was keen to declare that she would not fall in love where there was no hope of that love being returned. With M. Paul, the beginnings of what look like a special relationship have to be treated circumspectly in case the relationship should go wrong. By withholding information, Lucy does not leave herself exposed.

Another answer might have to do with context. This, as we have already noted, was a period in which women were not supposed to feel sexual desire. M. Paul's gifts to Lucy are courtship gifts. She, however, cannot allow herself to understand them as such until she is sure of his intentions; as a respectable nineteenth-century lady, she must not feel desire on her own behalf. Thus Lucy is hiding her emotions not just from us, but also from herself. The habits of self-restraint in which she has trained herself are very similar to what **psychoanalytic criticism** calls **repression**: that is, the process of forbidding oneself to think, feel or act on the grounds of desire.

CHAPTER 30   **M. Paul remains irascible. He teaches Lucy arithmetic, but their relationship is fraught**

Despite his mellowing, M. Paul is not easy to get along with. He undertakes to teach Lucy mathematics, and is initially gentle and encouraging. But as soon as she begins to make progress, he is as unreasonable as ever. On one occasion, Lucy is so offended that she throws his books at him and calls an end to the lessons, but he wheedles her back and the battles recommence. Another time, when Rosine, the portresse, interrupts a lesson to deliver an invitation from Dr John to a lecture and Lucy agrees, M. Paul is beside himself. He also tries to persuade her to submit to a public examination in composition in the next round of prize-giving. This horrifies Lucy and she refuses.

This extended study of M. Paul makes it very clear that he is far from a conventional hero. Bad-tempered, opinionated and flamboyant, he is often ungentlemanly in his treatment of Lucy and his other pupils. But, of course, if he is not a conventional hero, neither is Lucy a conventional heroine. What both fascinates and irritates M. Paul about Lucy is her will to think for herself. As a man trained in obedience by the Jesuit priests, with very strict views on the role of women, he is shocked that a woman might use her intellectual faculties to come to her own conclusions. Lucy doesn't like being bullied any more than M. Paul likes to be crossed; but she does like to watch people who are not predictable – so fascination is perhaps more important than irritation.

Madame de Stael French writer and renowned female intellectual (1766–1817)
Penthesilea a queen of the Amazons who fought on the Trojan (losing) side during the Trojan Wars
charity-schoolboy charity schools were set up for the children of the poor, and the quality of the education in them was variable, to say the least
Eutychus in Acts 20:9–12 Eutychus goes to sleep and falls out of a loft while listening to St Paul preaching. Miraculously, however, he is later found alive and unscathed
Hymettus a range of hills near Athens; the flowers of Hymettus are the benefits of a classical education
lusus naturae trick or wonder of nature
sound and fury, signifying nothing from Shakespeare's *Macbeth*, V.v
Baal ... Dagon Baal is an ancient Middle Eastern god of storms; Dagon, his son, is the god of fertility and grain

CHAPTER 31   **Lucy meets M. Paul in the garden. While talking, they are interrupted by the 'ghostly' nun**

One Sunday, when Lucy takes a nap in a classroom, she wakes to find that someone has covered her with a shawl. Later, while walking in the

ιe decides to save her money and establish a school of her own
.

She bumps into M. Paul (who had covered her up when she was
sleeping) and, again, he offers advice about her conduct. He also tells her
that he has a study overlooking the convent garden, so he knows the
goings-on of the house and is able to judge the real characters of its
inmates. Lucy declares his secret watching horrible, but is disarmed by his
admission that he too has seen the nun. At that moment, the branches of
the old pear tree begin to shake, though there is no wind, and the figure
of the nun passes them at speed.

What worries Lucy about her life is stagnation. She is ambitious to
make her way in the world, but the goal she sets herself – to run her
own school – does not wholly satisfy her:

> But … is there nothing more for me in life – no true home – nothing dearer to me
> than myself, and by its paramount preciousness, to draw from me better things
> than I care to culture for myself only? Nothing, at whose feet I can willingly lay
> down the whole burden of human egotism, and gloriously take up the nobler
> charge of labouring for others? (pp. 450–1)

She wants a true home: a husband and children – love – rather than
a career alone. While she wonders about love, M. Paul arrives,
foreshadowing the importance of their relationship.

Although M. Paul is, as usual, bad-tempered, this is nearly a proper
courtship scene. He has given signs of tender feelings towards Lucy
by covering her while she slept; now he accosts her alone – in an era
where male–female meetings were always supposed to be
chaperoned. And although he preaches, he also makes a kind of
declaration. He tells Lucy that he is not a marrying man, but he also
declares that he recognises her as a kindred spirit:

> … I was conscious of rapport between you and myself. You are patient, and I am
> choleric; you are quiet and pale, and I am tanned and fiery; you are a strict
> Protestant, and I am a sort of lay Jesuit: but we are alike – there is affinity. Do you
> see it, mademoiselle, when you look in the glass? (p. 457)

The moment is interrupted by the arrival of the nun – yet another
occasion when she appears at a time of heightened emotion.

Dryad a wood nymph

CHAPTER 32   Lucy meets Polly, who expresses her love for Dr John

Lucy bumps into Polly in Villette and is invited to spend the following evening with her. Polly confides that she has received a love letter from Dr John. She had replied to it with great difficulty, saying that while she liked him, she could not maintain a correspondence without her father's knowledge and permission. Lucy praises her self-control and tells her simply to wait. Her father, who still thinks of her as a child, will come round.

One of Lucy's constant pains in the novel is to see the people she cares for fall in love with unworthy figures. Her opposition to Ginevra's flirtation with the doctor, for example, is not just about the propriety of a young girl flirting with a man for whom she feels nothing; it is also to do with her instinct that pain is being deliberately inflicted on Dr John. Polly, however, is a very different case, and Lucy is not jealous of her. She says of the young girl:

> I liked her. It is not a declaration I have often made concerning my acquaintance, in the course of this book ... Intimate intercourse, close inspection, disclosed in Paulina only what was delicate, intelligent, and sincere; therefore my regard for her lay deep. (p. 461)

These are Lucy's ideals of femininity: delicacy, intelligence and sincerity. They are mental attributes rather than physical ones (though delicacy may be, of course, both mental and physical), and are consistent with Lucy's disapproval of judgements based only on appearance. They are virtues that she finds lacking among her pupils. Although Polly needs to confess her love, it is not a boast, but a confession born of anxiety that she should behave properly to both her father and her beloved. It is her delicacy towards the feelings of others rather than her physical delicacy of which Lucy truly approves.

CHAPTER 33   The school goes on an outing to celebrate M. Paul's birthday; he seeks out Lucy's company all day

On May Day M. Paul commands the boarders and staff of the school to celebrate his birthday by accompanying him on a walk into the countryside. He is in excellent spirits, chatting to all, but Lucy is anxious to avoid him since she is wearing a new pink dress and is afraid of his comments. When he sees her dress, he teases her about it, but is not severe. Following breakfast at a local farm, the girls run off to play in the meadows, while Lucy sits at M. Paul's side and reads to him while he smokes.

Having established that she is content in his company, he asks her if she would be sad if he had to go away, and he calls her 'little sister'. Lucy is overcome with emotion. Later, back at school, she sees M. Paul in earnest conversation with Madame Beck and knows that he is sad. When he comes to find her, she runs away.

> At last we are beginning to get more than vague hints of the relationship between Lucy and M. Paul. It is clear from quite early in the novel that the professor singles her out for his particular attention. On his birthday outing, that notice is made more explicit. The endearment of *petite soeur* (little sister) is hardly a declaration of unbridled passion, but it *is* an endearment. The questions and hints that M. Paul might have to go away, and his attempts to ascertain Lucy's feeling for him, all point at the possibility of love.

collyrium soothing eye ointment

CHAPTER 34   **Lucy goes on an errand to Madame Walravens's house; there she meets Père Silas again and hears the story of M. Paul's life**

One day, as a storm is brewing, Lucy is sent by Madame Beck to deliver a basket of fruit to Madame Walravens, and to ensure that she sees the old lady personally. She is shown into a dark room, where she is drawn to the outline of a picture which suddenly seems to move. In fact, it conceals a door through which a hideous old woman – Madame Walravens – appears. Lucy delivers her gift and message, and the old lady is very rude. Lucy leaves her and waits on the landing for the rain to stop. There, an old priest finds her and invites her back to the salon. Lucy realises that this is Père Silas, the priest to whom she had turned for help.

Lucy's eyes are drawn to the picture that moved and she sees that it depicts a young nun. The priest tells her that this woman was much beloved, and is missed by no one so much as her fiancé. His former pupil, now his benefactor, had been in love with her, but when his father's business failed, the engagement was broken off by the girl's proud family: indeed, her grandmother, Madame Walravens, had been most insistent. The girl – Justine-Marie – died in a convent and the lover was heartbroken. None the less, when Justine-Marie's own family fell on hard times, the fiancé took in the girl's grandmother, despite the fact that she had ruined his life. He also housed the priest and an old servant, using most of his income in their support, making it impossible that he should ever marry. At the end of this narrative Lucy suddenly becomes suspicious that there is some hidden purpose to the errand and the story. The priest goes on to tell her that the benefactor in question is none other than M. Paul.

Lucy returns home and reports what happened to Madame Beck. The headmistress casually reiterates what Lucy has already heard: that M. Paul is too charitable for his own good and can never marry.

> This episode has many attributes of a fairy story. Like Little Red Riding Hood, Lucy sets off carrying a basket and with strict instructions. Madame Walravens, while not a wolf in old lady's clothes, is certainly wolf-like in her fierceness. Lucy explicitly links her to the world of fairy stories, referring to her as Malevola (the traditional name for the bad fairy in 'Sleeping Beauty') and as Cunegonde, a hideously deformed woman in Voltaire's *Candide* (1759). Her dwarfish stature, her hunched back and her association with riches all echo the evil symbols found in children's tales. In some ways more worrying, though, is the sense that Lucy has become embroiled in a plot hatched by Père Silas and Madame Beck. (Jesuit priests are made to seem even more frightening and sinister than Madame Walravens.) Even the accident of the bad weather conspires to make Lucy linger and hear the tale of M. Paul's love and loss. The whole chapter is another example of the **Gothic** atmosphere that pervades the novel. These events are calculated to unsettle Lucy's certainties, and the concerted attack on the idea of M. Paul marrying is also highly significant.

Tadmor   a city built in the Wilderness by Solomon (II Chronicles 8:4)

Sidonia   a sorceress in Greek mythology

pax vobiscum   Latin phrase meaning 'peace be with you'

CHAPTER 35   Lucy is forced to take a public examination. Later, she and the professor re-pledge their friendship

The next day, M. Paul forces Lucy to undergo an examination of her intellectual abilities by two professors at the boys' college. Lucy cannot answer any of the questions set by her hostile interrogators, so M. Paul is disappointed and the professors think her an idiot. Giving her one last chance, they ask her to write an essay on the subject of 'Human Justice'. At first, Lucy cannot think of anything to write; then she suddenly recognises the two professors as the men who had chased her on her first night in Villette. She is suddenly inspired and writes a powerful essay.

When Lucy next sees M. Paul, she quarrels with him for this forced examination. Later again, though, they meet more calmly in the garden. Lucy asks M. Paul about himself, then tells him about her visit to Madame Walravens and what she has learned from Père Silas. This results in M. Paul requesting that they be like brother and sister to each other – good friends, able to rely on each other for consolation and advice.

As we know, Lucy spends a great deal of time watching and judging the actions of others, and she is generally dissatisfied that others pay too much attention to outward appearance. The subject of 'Human Justice' for her essay, therefore, is a chance to write of her own philosophy. Human justice, based as it usually is on improperly considered human judgements, is not justice at all. She portrays justice as a woman, but without the usual females virtues. It is:

a red, random beldame with arms akimbo. I saw her in her house, the den of confusion: servants called to her for orders or help which she did not give; beggars stood at her door waiting and starving unnoticed; a swarm of children, sick and quarrelsome crawled round her feet and yelled in her ears appeals for notice, sympathy, cure, redress. (p. 495)

Lucy's choice of a female image is instructive. Over and over again she has watched men judge women by their appearances, and fail to comprehend that a pretty face is not the same thing at all as a decent person. Her image of a woman indifferent to human suffering is a moral antidote to the images of female virtue Lucy had been presented with in the art gallery (Chapter 19). As such, it is not only a rebuke to the two gentlemen sitting in judgement on her intellectual prowess, but yet another assertion of her independence from M. Paul's views about ideal womanhood.

It was, of course, M. Paul who had made her look at the four pictures of a woman's life in the gallery: thinking back to the portrait of Justine-Marie, Lucy comments:

> I knew what she was as well as if I had seen her ... If she wore angels' wings, I knew whose poet-fancy conferred them. If her forehead shone luminous with the reflex of a halo, I knew in the fire of whose irids that circlet of holy flame had generation. (p. 491)

In other words, M. Paul has *made* Justine-Marie an angel. In her own right, she is an ordinary girl. The critique that Lucy mounts here is to do with the ways in which people (but especially men) judge others (especially women) by impossible standards.

Messieurs Boissec and Rochemorte literally Mister Drywood and Mister Deadrock

there was a crow to pluck another way of saying 'a bone to pick'

CHAPTER 36   **M. Paul seems distant, despite his promise of friendship**

M. Paul seems to be avoiding Lucy, but when she opens her desk, she discovers that he has left her a pamphlet written by Père Silas urging Protestants to convert to Catholicism. Lucy reads it with indifference, but she realises that M. Paul's distance is the result of religious differences, not because he has gone off her.

When she has finished reading, she spots M. Paul in the garden. He asks her opinion of the tract. Lucy tells him that she is unimpressed, and they go on to have a serious discussion about religion and its meaning in their two lives. This conversation is, of course, reported by M. Paul to his confessor, Père Silas, who comes to the school himself to try to convert Lucy. He is unsuccessful. M. Paul, at least, understands that he and she worship the same God, utter the same prayers and have the same ethical frameworks, even if the details of worship differ.

This chapter constitutes the clearest statement in *Villette* of Lucy's anti-Catholicism. For her, the Catholic Church is an evil institution because of its insistence on regular worship rather than moral rectitude. Much earlier in the novel (Chapter 9), Lucy had commented in shock that the Catholic girls she teaches have no compunction about telling lies and think that reading a novel or missing church are more serious sins. For her, on the other hand, failing to go to church is far less important than telling a lie. Catholics, she feels, are hypocritical because they lie to themselves. The dogma of Catholic religion takes up too much time and effort that should be directed at self-examination and prayer. Protestantism, by contrast, leaves the worshipper more independent. As she says to M. Paul, 'we [Protestants] kept fewer forms between us and God' (p. 516). If Lucy seeks spiritual guidance, she reads the Bible for herself and comes to her own conclusions rather than living by ready-made doctrine. Catholicism is based on unquestioning obedience, not on intellect or self-discipline, she argues, and it is therefore unacceptable to her.

St Vincent de Paul French priest and philanthropist (*c*.1581–1660), famous for charitable works, such as the founding of hospitals and schools

the ruddy old lady of the seven hills the Catholic Church is sometimes referred to as the old lady of Rome, which is built on seven hills

more honoured in the breach than in the observance from Shakespeare's *Hamlet*, I.iv

CHAPTER 37   **Polly and Dr John become engaged**

Although the courtship between Polly and Dr John is proceeding, Polly is distressed that her father still knows nothing of it. One day, however, after Dr John has dined with the family and Lucy, Polly's father questions Lucy about what is going on. He is distressed and tells Lucy that he cannot imagine a life without his daughter. Lucy acts as advocate for the lovers, attesting to their love and impeccable behaviour. She realises that M. de Bassompierre does not wish his daughter ever to marry. Polly herself then enters the room, intending to show Lucy a letter she has written to Dr John. She nervously hands the letter to her father instead, and confesses her feelings for the doctor. The old man is very upset.

When Dr John returns from a call, Lucy warns him of the scene that is unfolding. At first M. de Bassompierre's remarks are teasing and uncomfortable, but eventually the older man takes the younger man away to his study to discuss the matter, and when they come back, it is settled that Polly and Dr John are engaged.

A few days later Lucy sees Polly weaving together some strands of her father's and her lover's hair with a lock of her own as a charm against them ever falling out. Their lives, Lucy says, are blessed. The young couple marry and enjoy the good things of life. They were made to be happy, and they live up to their early promise.

When Lucy looks at Polly and Dr John, she recognises them as people who are both materially and constitutionally better off than she – people for whom happiness is possible. Her commentary on their lives leads to a direct contrast with her own emptier existence. Watching a couple in love emphasises the lack of such feelings for Lucy herself, not least because she has harboured unrequited romantic emotions for Dr John.

Throughout the novel, Polly has been presented to the reader as a child. Even now she is eighteen, her father still sees her as a little girl. **Psychoanalytic** approaches to literature would regard this as highly significant, since the Victorians considered eighteen a marriageable age for a wealthy woman – an age of sexual maturity. Her father, however, sees the girl as asexual, incapable of desire because she is too young. Indeed, he views her as his possession: precious, but inert; valued, but with no will of her own – 'My little jewel,' he calls her, 'the only pearl I have' (p. 522). Polly understands this and plays on her father's perception of her childishness in the scene where she persuades him of the sincerity of her affection for Dr John. By playing the child, she does not force him to confront the desire that motivates her love. This tactic also allows him to seem more powerful, and to grant her wish as a kind of indulgence to a little girl, not as the right of a grown woman.

braw　Scots dialect for 'brave'
Pentelicus　a mountain near Athens which has famous marble quarries
Rachel weeping for her children　Jeremiah 31:15, a reference to the boys aged under two killed by Herod

CHAPTER 38   **M. Paul is to leave Europe on family business. Madame Beck and Père Silas keep Lucy and the professor apart; Madame even resorts to drugging her, but Lucy gets up in the middle of the night and joins the crowds at the city fair while under the influence of opium**

One day, Madame Beck announces that M. Paul is leaving to make a long visit to the West Indies on family business. Lucy is desolate.

On M. Paul's last day, Madame Beck asks Lucy to translate an English letter, shutting her into a room with exaggerated care. This makes Lucy suspicious, so when she hears a noise, she leaves the room, despite Madame's protests, and finds the professor making his farewells to the school. Madame, however, prevents her cousin from seeing Lucy and hurries him away. Later Lucy receives a note from M. Paul saying that he has important news for her and will see her alone before he sails. Knowing he is to sail the next day, Lucy waits for him in the classroom all evening, but he does not come. Madame Beck tries to persuade her to bed, and there is a confrontation between them. Lucy realises that the headmistress is her rival for M. Paul. The next day she is given a powerful sedative on Madame Beck's orders.

The drug does not have the intended effect: Lucy is stimulated rather than sedated. She goes for a walk in the park and is surprised to find it filled with people enjoying a carnival. She catches sight of the Brettons and Bassompierres in the crowd and follows them, but the crowd carries her off to a different spot. She finds herself near Madame Beck and her family: among the party are Père Silas and Madame Walravens.

The title of this chapter, 'Cloud', reflects the contrast between Lucy's shadowy existence and the sun-filled fortunes of Polly and Dr John. It also describes the way in which Lucy feels she is being kept 'in the dark' and is 'under a cloud' in relation to M. Paul's planned departure. 'Cloud' also **alludes** to the state of Lucy's mind under the influence of laudanum (opium dissolved in alcohol – a common sedative in the nineteenth century). In her clouded brain, the park appears to be a dreamscape:

In a land of enchantment, a garden most gorgeous, a plain sprinkled with
coloured meteors, a forest with sparks of purple and ruby and golden fire
gemming the foliage; a region, not of trees and shadow, but of the strangest
architectural wealth – of altar and temple, of pyramid and obelisk, and sphynx;
incredible to say, the wonders and the symbols of Egypt teemed throughout the
park of Villette. (p. 550)

It is perhaps no surprise that the prosaic Lucy immediately
identifies the way the illusion has been made, with 'timber ... paint
... pasteboard' (p. 550), and brings the hallucinatory world back to
earth with a bang. The question of illusion and reality has, of
course, been a prominent theme in the novel so far. Here we have
a scene that appears absolutely illusory, but is in fact real and solid,
despite appearances. Just as judging people by appearances is
unreliable, so one cannot judge experience merely by how it looks.

an Alnaschar dream an impossible dream. In *The Arabian Nights*, Alnaschar
is a merchant who buys glassware. Before he can sell it, it gets broken and
he loses all his money

a Jean-Jacques sensibility Jean-Jacques Rousseau (1712–78), a French
philosopher famed for his emphasis on the innocence of sincere emotion

Peri-Banou a peri is an Eastern version of a fairy or sprite. In *The Arabian
Nights*, Peri-Banou has a tent that can be held in one hand but which also
has infinite dimensions

CHAPTER 39   Lucy discovers that M. Paul has not yet sailed. He
arrives to join the party, and Lucy flees. On her
return to the school, she discovers the nun in her bed

As Lucy gazes on the Beck party in the park, she tells us what she has
learned about M. Paul's departure. Madame Walravens is the owner of a
West Indian estate only recently freed from creditors. Now it needs
careful management to bring it into profit. Père Silas and Madame Beck
have decided that M. Paul is the best person to undertake this task – and
it will keep him away from Lucy.

Lucy overhears Madame Walravens ask when Justine-Marie is
to arrive. That is the name of the dead nun beloved by M. Paul. When
M. Paul arrives with Justine-Marie, Lucy recognises her as an ordinary

Villette girl and a relative of Mesdames Beck and Walravens. She is jealous of what appears to be love between M. Paul and the girl. As she listens, she learns that M. Paul has deferred his departure in order to complete some business before he goes. On the way back to school a carriage passes and someone appears to wave a handkerchief at her from the window.

When she gets to her room, Lucy finds someone in her bed – the figure of a nun. She discovers that it is simply a bolster dressed in a nun's habit. A pencilled note on the pillow announces that the nun will be seen no more. Lucy hides all the evidence and goes to bed.

This chapter continues the theme of appearance and reality. Lucy is convinced of her own unlovability by long experience, so watching the affection between M. Paul and Justine-Marie reinforces that conviction. Although glad to see M. Paul, her emotions are painfully mixed. She speaks of jealousy as 'a vulture ... strong in beak and talon' (pp. 566–7). She feels her hopes of being loved have been betrayed, but yet again she is deceived by appearances.

On her return to the school she is forced to confront another 'appearance', this time the figure of the nun. Where once it had made her doubt her own sanity and stability, this time she has a different response to it:

I could afford neither consternation, scream nor swoon. Besides, I was not overcome. Tempered by late incidents, my nerves disdained hysteria. Warm from illuminations, and music, and thronging thousands, thoroughly lashed up by a new scourge, I defied spectra. (p. 569)

Her previous encounters with the nun had taken place when she was feeling lonely and distanced from human experience. This episode takes place when her life is much fuller, so she has the courage to confront her demons. Of course, the mystery of the nun has not yet been resolved, but it is definitely not a phantom, so now there is nothing to fear.

Paul et Virginie the title characters of a sentimental novel by Bernadin de St Pierre (1787)

Rosinante Don Quixote's horse in the satirical romance *Don Quixote de la Mancha* by Miguel de Cervantes (1547–1616)

CHAPTER 40   A schoolgirl disappears and an elopement is
              discovered

The following morning Ginevra has disappeared. Lucy guesses that she
has eloped with Alfred de Hamal – the waving handkerchief from the
speeding carriage she had seen the previous night must have been
Ginevra. She tells Madame Beck her suspicions, and M. de Bassompierre
sets out in pursuit of the couple, but finds them too late to stop the
marriage. A few days later Lucy receives a letter from Ginevra telling
her about the elopement, and explaining that the nun was, in fact, her
dear Alfred in disguise so that he could visit her. Despite M. de
Bassompierre's disapproval, he gives Ginevra a dowry and finds Alfred a
diplomatic job. The couple lead a feckless life, contracting debts because
they live beyond their means. However, they seem happy enough, and
have definitely not been punished for extravagance and irresponsibility.

It has always been a mystery that Lucy should get on so well
with Ginevra. It seems that she admires her honesty, if not her
shallowness, and envies her ability to be happy and carefree.
Whatever the explanation, the narrative here does not punish
Ginevra for the highly improper act of elopement. Nor does Lucy
seem to hold a grudge for having been nearly frightened to death by
the 'ghostly' nun.

détournement de mineur corruption of a minor. The age of adulthood in
Victorian England was twenty-one, and Ginevra is only eighteen

CHAPTER 41   M. Paul visits Lucy before he sails and shows her a
              school he has procured for her to run; he loves her
              and plans to marry her when he returns from
              Guadaloupe

Lucy has virtually given up all hope of seeing M. Paul again. He comes,
however, and insists on seeing her alone, despite Madame Beck's
resistance. He takes her to a pretty house in a quiet suburb and reveals
that one of the rooms is a classroom. He proposes that Lucy should be its
headmistress while he is away. She discovers that she already has two
pupils in the daughters of her landlord, but is dismayed when M. Paul
asks her to teach English to Justine-Marie. She reveals what she has seen

in the park and the professor seems gratified by her jealousy. He spells out his plan for the future: that when he returns from Guadaloupe, he will marry Lucy Snowe.

Much earlier in the novel Ginevra had asked Lucy, 'Who *are* you, Miss Snowe?' and received the answer: 'Who am I indeed? Perhaps a personage in disguise. Pity I don't look the character' (p. 393). Lucy is jokingly referring to the conventions of **romantic fiction**, where beautiful but disguised ladies and gentlemen are stock features, but true to her realistic assessment of life, she also declares that she does not look the part. In this chapter, as the novel reaches its **denouement**, Lucy at last gets her opportunity to play the romantic heroine. Her hero is not exactly tall, dark and handsome; nor does he have the suave manners usually associated with lovers in fiction. None the less, it is important to her to be told that she is desirable. Lucy – strict with herself as ever – does not approve of her own vanity on this point, but she cannot help asking M. Paul:

'Do I displease your eyes *much*?' … He stopped, and gave me a short, strong answer – an answer which silenced, subdued, yet profoundly satisfied. Ever after that, I knew what I was for *him*; and what I might be for the rest of the world, I ceased painfully to care. Was it weak to lay so much stress on an opinion about appearance? I fear it might be – I fear it was; but in that case I must avow no light share of weakness. I must own a great fear of displeasing – a strong wish moderately to please M. Paul. (p. 583)

The precise details of M. Paul's answer are withheld from the reader in the kind of teasing omission that we have come to expect. But this is clearly the language of romantic fiction: his 'short, strong answer' and her response in silence, subjugation and satisfaction are exactly the terms one might expect in a more conventional romance when the heroine falls into the hero's arms. Lucy gets her romantic moment.

Polchinelle Pulchinello, or Punch

CHAPTER 42   **M. Paul leaves Lucy, perhaps never to return**

The years of M. Paul's absence are paradoxically the happiest of Lucy's life since she is occupied, useful and working for a purpose – the hope of a future with M. Paul. Her school prospers, and her spirits are kept up by regular letters from her beloved.

At last the three years of absence are over and M. Paul is to return. Perhaps his boat is sunk on the voyage, but Lucy will not spoil our hopes for her happiness by telling us. Instead, her last words are to say that Madame Beck and Père Silas prosper, and that Madame Walravens lived to be ninety before she died.

We noted earlier that Lucy prefers to travel than to arrive, relishing anticipation rather than fulfilment. This final chapter makes that point once again. Lucy is happy waiting for her lover because she is waiting for a dream to come true. We will never see the dream fulfilled – and she seems almost to prefer the dream than to test out the reality of her romantic expectations in the everyday world.

The ending of this novel is at once abrupt and **ambiguous**. We are given unnecessary news of characters for whom we care little, while the fate of a much more important character is left unresolved. Lucy tells us that we are free to imagine her happiness, but the images of the final paragraphs – shipwreck (the metaphor of the sea making its final appearance), bad winter weather, and the continued success of those who had plotted against her and M. Paul – make us unlikely to do so. The hints are very strong that M. Paul will never return. Yet Lucy is not a tragic figure at the end of her story. She has a function and role in life. Unlike the pretty women in other parts of the book, she is more than a physical appearance and a set of contingent social circumstances. She has made herself and her own worth. These circumstances make it unimportant that she does not marry in the end because she knows that she has been loved.

PART THREE

CRITICAL APPROACHES

CHARACTERISATION

The characters of *Villette* are complex rather than straightforward. One of the novel's key themes is that of the relationships between appearance and reality, and this theme is played out in detail in relation to characters, who are seldom what they first appear. We often presume that we know a literary character more thoroughly than we would a real one, and we expect consistency in literary characterisation. Above all, we expect characters to keep the same names throughout a fiction, the names being the key typographical markers of their identities. In this novel, however, characterisation often seems inconsistent. Indeed, many characters are described as having at least two personalities – one for public view, one for private. And at least two significant characters appear under more than one name. The novel takes it as given that human beings are sometimes unfathomable.

LUCY SNOWE

Lucy's character is elusive. Despite the fact that the novel is largely concerned with her life and emotions, much information is missing. She never, for example, gives us an explicit description of her physical appearance. We can surmise that she is small and plain from the few remarks she makes about herself. Her physical attributes are figured in absence and disguise. She says of herself: 'I had a staid manner of my own which ere now had been as good to me as a cloak and hood of hodden gray' (p. 104). This comment is typical – the grey cloak and hood help her to hide; she makes a point of not drawing attention to herself and is almost always discomfited when she attracts anyone's notice. In addition to not revealing what she looks like, Lucy also withholds the kinds of information that might be thought of as the mainstay of **autobiographical fiction**. We are not told about her family or how she was orphaned; we know nothing of her childhood, education, or social status. Sometimes she even wilfully misleads her readers, as when she tells us to imagine that she had a happy life between leaving Bretton and arriving at Miss Marchmont's house (Chapter 4), and as when she refuses to tell us that Dr John and Graham Bretton are the same person. In short, her narrative, like her character, is devious rather than straightforward.

As with most of the other characters, Lucy is also inconsistent. For example, the careful reader will be only too aware of her feelings for Dr John, but Lucy herself denies these feelings. The calm, cool exterior and self-control that she cultivates (she is not called 'Snowe' for nothing) are in fact merely a veneer. Underneath, Lucy seethes with unrequited passions, demonstrated in the two sets of letters she writes to Dr John, and in the violence of the biblical imagery she uses to describe how she maintains her composure (Chapter 12). Other people call her a prude and a puritan because that is the impression she gives them. We know differently – we know that she is deeply emotional, thirsting for love, desperate for recognition even as she hides herself away. It makes Lucy a very uncomfortable heroine whose self-disclosure we cannot quite trust because we know that it is only partial.

DR JOHN/GRAHAM BRETTON

It is important that Dr John is known in the text by two different names. This indicates that he cannot be read at one go. The young Graham, whom we first meet at Bretton in the novel's early pages, seems a nice enough young man. We are given some details of his personal appearance, including the fact that he has red hair, yet is nonetheless attractive. He is also described as manly, in contrast to the effete Alfred de Hamal. He is making a career for himself, something of which both Lucy and most of her audience would have approved as a sign of proper masculinity. He is socially at ease and professionally competent. Yet despite all these positive attributes, we are also told in no uncertain terms that he is not perfect.

Lucy tells us that his public persona is everything one might wish of a professional young man: 'he is shown oblivious of self; as modest in the display of his energies, as earnest in their exercise' (p. 273). His private persona is more self-satisfied and complacent. In addition, Lucy regards him as a severe judge, particularly in his judgements of the women he loves. He is easily fooled by a pretty face such as Ginevra's. On the other hand, he does have the capacity for development. The effect on him of his love for Polly is very positive: 'All that was best in Graham sought Paulina; whatever in him was noble, awoke, and grew in her presence.' By the time we leave him, he no longer judges by appearance only, and his 'whole intellect, and his highest tastes' (p. 518) are engaged in his affection. He becomes the ideal, conventional lover in an ordinary **romantic fiction**. As such, he is the ideal lover of little Polly Home.

GINEVRA FANSHAWE

The oddity of her name immediately marks out this character. Ginevra derives from 'Guinevere', King Arthur's adulterous queen, so a connection is made with dubious romance. This is compounded by her surname; the fan was an object associated with flirtation and shallow emotion. Ginevra lives up to her name, being both pretty and heartless. Although Lucy disapproves of almost everything Ginevra does, she continues to like and tolerate her because Ginevra is fun and has the gift of enjoying herself without the interference of moral scruples – something that the repressed Lucy envies. In contrast to most of the other people Lucy meets, Ginevra is not at all complex. She is frankly out to enjoy her life, and in the often-hypocritical world of Villette, that frankness is a welcome change.

POLLY HOME/COUNTESS PAULINA HOME DE BASSOMPIERRE

Like her eventual husband, Polly also has more than one name. The accumulation of names, and the change from the diminutive 'Polly' to the grown-up 'Paulina' signals a growing maturity and a change in social circumstances. But it also indicates that Polly has more than one self. When we first meet her as a small child, there is something of the **uncanny** about her, 'haunting' the house at Bretton with her insubstantial presence. That sense of the fairy child is retained when Lucy meets her again in Villette, so there is continuity between the six-year-old Polly and her adult character. But Polly also deliberately plays different roles to different audiences. Her father believes her to be a little child because she plays that part when she is with him; with Lucy 'she was serious, and as womanly as thought and feeling could make her' (p. 384); with the learned men who visit her father, she is grave and intellectual. Her personality is not essence but a performance. This does not mean that she is untrustworthy or insincere; she is what the occasion requires – the perfect social being who responds surely to every context.

MADAME BECK

Lucy's view of Madame Beck is extremely ambivalent. On the one hand, the headmistress is a role model for her, being a professional woman making her way successfully in the world at a time when such achievement was usually confined to men. Her school is efficiently run and compares favourably with schools in England. At the same time, Lucy loathes Madame Beck's methods, which she associates with debased religious practice and lack of heart. The system of spying on staff and students alike to ensure their compliance with the rules of the house disgusts Lucy as an example of what happens when religious practice depends more on appearance than conscience. Madame Beck is governed by self-interest. The Catholicism she practises is less a matter of faith than convention: if the parents are Catholic, then the headmistress must appear to be Catholic as well to uphold the good reputation of the school. Nonetheless, having decided on her system, Madame Beck carries it out with absolute consistency. She moves around the school silently and gracefully, passing through well-oiled doors locked with well-oiled keys. Unlike other figures in the novel, she is described as 'a most consistent character; forbearing with all the world, and tender to no part of it' (p. 157). Her school runs like clockwork and her behaviour is similarly predictable.

Lucy can even find it in herself occasionally to feel sorry for Madame Beck, who, like all the women in the novel, is vulnerable to masculine judgements of feminine beauty. While she is professionally powerful and almost admirable, she is also disappointed by the evidence of her fading physical charms, and has to make enormous efforts to disguise and conquer her feelings for Dr John. Lucy's final judgement of her, though, is excoriating. Her lack of tenderness even to her own children is a symptom of Madame's fatal flaw: she has no heart and can imagine no motivation apart from material advantage. She interferes in Lucy's relationship with M. Paul because her self-interest dictates that she should either marry him herself, or prevent him from marrying (and thus taking his wealth) outside the family. Because Lucy values the importance of passion and feelings, Madame Beck's absolutely rational personality is finally harshly judged.

MONSIEUR PAUL EMMANUEL

Paul Emmanuel is an unconventional hero for a love story. He is not tall, dark and handsome; he is not even well-mannered. His attentions to Lucy produce equal pleasure and horror in her, and it takes him a very long time to declare himself her lover at all. Indeed, his character attacks the very idea of convention in every way: he storms and rails at Lucy, assailing Victorian conventions of polite relations between the sexes; he criticises her appearance and clothing, breaking the taboos on making personal remarks and commenting adversely on a beloved's appearance. He allows himself to be mastered by petty irritation, but is perversely noble when real difficulties present themselves. In his attitudes to Père Silas and Madame Walravens, and in his sense of duty towards family obligations, he is almost saintly. His religious beliefs are sincerely held, and he lives by his faith. But what renders him loveable to Lucy is the fact that he pays her serious (if often uncomfortable) attention. There are the little gifts of books and chocolates placed in her desk; there is also the intellectual commitment to her – he teaches her subjects in which she is ignorant. And he is the only male in the novel who actually *looks* at her, even if he is often unflattering. His assumptions about Lucy when he first meets her are that she is just an ordinary, conventional girl. When he discovers that she has a mind of her own, he is attracted to the challenge she represents to his **stereotyped** notions of **femininity**. His final gift to her – the faith that she can independently and efficiently run the school he has procured for her – is testament to his intelligence and sensitivity. What he eventually gives Lucy is a relationship based on equality of mind, not on the superficialities of appearance. He is a new kind of romantic hero: not strong and silent, but intuitive and voluble; not handsome but ordinary; not perfect but a good match for Lucy's own equally unconventional virtues.

APPEARANCE AND REALITY

One of the key interests of *Villette* is its exploration of the mismatch between appearance and reality. Seeing and knowledge are often taken to be interdependent: 'I see' can also mean 'I understand'. In this text, however, appearances are deceptive. The novel mounts a sustained attack on the easy judgements that are made without thought. Dr John, for example, is a fool when he sees Ginevra's pretty face and presumes that she is an angel. Mr Home is misled by Polly's appearance of childishness, which belies her growing maturity. The conflict between appearance and reality is intimately related to Lucy Snowe's sense of her own inferior physical attributes. She knows that she is not pretty, but she also knows that she is not worthless. Her aim, therefore, is to demonstrate that appearances alone are not an adequate basis for judgement. She is particularly disturbed that men judge women by appearance, as if a woman's sole worth is in her looks. Seeing is unreliable, Lucy argues, because it is subjective. Speaking of herself, she says:

> What contradictory attributes of character we sometimes find ascribed to us, *according to the eye with which we are viewed!* Madame Beck esteemed me learned and blue; Miss Fanshawe, caustic, ironic, and cynical; Mr Home, a model teacher, the essence of the sedate and discreet ... whilst ... Professor Paul Emmanuel ... never lost an opportunity of intimating his opinion that mine was rather a fiery and rash nature – adventurous, indocile, and audacious. (p. 386)

This multiplicity of view would not matter were it not for the fact that each person's eye presumes its own particular point of view is correct; people do not perceive complexity or ambiguity as the attributes of others.

SPYING

The second kind of seeing in the novel – spying – avoids making eye contact with others. In fact, the person doing it tries to avoid being seen at all. It is used to find out secrets and to discover if appearance and reality match. This is Madame Beck's activity above all, and she is very good at it. Spying, of course, is unpleasant, conveying distrust and suspicion, both of which Madame Beck feels in abundance. But the novel's attitude to this process is nonetheless ambivalent. After all, when Madame spies on Lucy, Lucy spies back. She knows that her things have been examined, has watched Madame through half-closed eyelids and has caught her in the act on other occasions. There is, however, no confrontation between Lucy and Madame Beck. Thus both a character with whom we sympathise and one whom we dislike carry out furtive acts of espionage.

RELIGION

Victorian fiction often betrays an interest in religion that is alien to present-day readers. Charlotte Brontë was the daughter of a clergyman, so it is no surprise that her novel is littered with quotations from and **allusions** to the Bible. But *Villette* also betrays a zealous interest in religious politics, particularly in the rival claims of Roman Catholicism and the Church of England to represent true religion. Lucy Snowe's antipathy to Catholicism can be traced to the historical background of the novel. The thirty years that preceded the publication of *Villette* had been very turbulent years for religious faith in England. In 1828 the Test Act (which 'tested' the Anglican faith of holders of public office) was repealed; a year later the Catholic Emancipation Act overturned the sixteenth-century law that prevented Catholics from holding public office. By 1850, the Roman Catholic hierarchy of cardinals and bishops had been re-established in England. These facts were alarming to members of the Established Church of England. In addition, the Church of England had its own internal divisions made public. An evangelical wing, which emphasised the personal relationship between the believer and God, was at odds with the Tractarian (or Oxford) Movement, a High Church (or quasi-Catholic) movement, which called for renewed commitment to the Church's strict hierarchy. In addition, there was a Broad Church movement, which emphasised tolerance for diversity of religious conscience within the broad framework of the Established Church.

Lucy's version of Christianity is a combination of evangelical and Broad Church principles. Her faith is based on her own readings of the Bible, unmediated by any priest, and on her own conclusions about morality and practice. The virtues of this system, she suggests, are tolerance (she does not seek to convert anyone to her point of view); honesty – she has to examine her own conscience and cannot lie to herself (whereas the Catholic girls she teaches are always lying); self-imposed discipline and self-restraint (as opposed to the necessity for spying on girls who have not learned to govern their own behaviour); and absence of hypocrisy (Lucy's faith does not depend on forms of worship and dogma, as she argues Catholicism does). She associates these virtues not only with her own religious faith, but also with Englishness – it's not for nothing that her church is the Church of *England* – and they are contrasted with the sneaky ways of the foreigners with whom she is surrounded.

Only at her weakest is Lucy tempted by Catholicism. When, in Chapter 15, she visits Père Silas's confessional, she seeks the relief of human contact, but she is also attracted by surrender: to her mind, becoming a Catholic would mean no longer having to think for herself. This is attractive only for a moment because she sees submission to the Roman Church as a kind of annihilation: 'As soon should I have thought of walking in the Babylonish furnace' (p. 235). Her personality as well as her religion demand self-reliance, not surrender. Thus, when Père Silas and M. Paul both try later to convert her, they stand no chance of success. It is not just her faith at stake, but also her nationality and personality.

EDUCATION

A novel set in a girls' school is obviously in part about female education. Brontë herself had worked as a governess and as a schoolteacher, and had even dreamed of establishing her own school. In *Jane Eyre* she had described the horrors of a school where the pupils were badly treated, having insufficient food, poor clothing and bad housing. At Madame Beck's school, these abuses are absent, and the girls are well fed and healthy. But, through Lucy, scathing condemnations are made about the curriculum offered to bourgeois women:

> Severe or continuous mental application they could not, or would not, bear: heavy demand on the memory, the reason, the attention, they rejected point-blank. Where an English girl of not more than average capacity and docility, would

quietly take a theme and bind herself to the task of comprehension and mastery, a Labasscourienne would laugh in your face, and throw it back to you with the phrase – 'Dieu que c'est difficile! Je n'en veux pas. Cela m'ennuie trop.' (p. 146)

To Lucy's mind, the girls learn nothing at school. There are showy displays of learning on prize-giving day, but they are not real. The pupils at Madame Beck's are mostly destined for the marriage market, so they need to know nothing much and will not have to use their learning to earn their own livings. So long as they are decorative and compliant, the school has done its work.

Lucy's own case is different. For her, knowledge is the key to independence. She applies herself to her studies because she has to if she wishes to fulfil her dream of opening her own school. Lucy's education at the hands of M. Paul, though, is not just a matter of formal instruction; it is also what we might call a 'sentimental education', in which she learns about feeling and love. There is an erotic charge between the teacher and his pupil: he is powerful (a conventionally masculine trait) and she is weak (a conventionally feminine one). Their lessons are among the few occasions when they occupy these conventional roles, and their love flourishes during them.

IMAGERY AND SYMBOLISM

SEA IMAGERY AND THE ABSENCE OF HOME

There is a sense in which we must understand Lucy as a figure of the **uncanny**. In his essay on *unheimlich* (uncanny) effects in literature, the psychoanalyst Sigmund Freud pointed out that the German word means literally 'unhomely' – the uncanny is that which 'haunts' a home, but has no home of its own. This describes Lucy's situation: she has no place of her own until the end of the novel, when she is ensconced in her new school. Her almost childish delight in its simple furnishings bespeaks the fact that she has been unable to call these things her own for most of her life. Her lack of place, whether physical or social, means that she is a character who is often 'all at sea'.

At the beginning of Chapter 4, Lucy describes her life as a kind of sea journey, and asks the reader to picture her 'as a bark slumbering

through halcyon weather' (p. 94). We can guess, however, that she does
not mean us to believe that her life was in fact calm or ideal. In any case,
that period is soon over and 'there must have been a wreck at last'. The
metaphor of the shipwreck was very much more potent for the Victorians
than for present-day readers. The shipwreck was the nineteenth-century
equivalent of a plane crash – a disaster in which there was virtually no
chance of survival. The metaphor expresses more anguish than we might
notice.

After Miss Marchmont's death, Lucy really does find herself at sea
on a real voyage. This is a time of strange excitement for her. Although
unnerved by the journey – 'I thought of the Styx and of Charon rowing
some solitary soul to the Land of Shades' (p. 111) – once aboard the ship
she feels relatively calm until she thinks of the future:

> Some difficulties had been passed through; a sort of victory was won: my homeless,
> anchorless, unsupported mind had again leisure for a brief repose: till the 'Vivid'
> arrived in harbour, no further action would be required of me, but then ... Oh! I
> could not look forward. (p. 112)

The turbulence of Lucy's mind, conveyed through nautical imagery,
shows how she is perversely more 'at home' when she is 'all at sea'. She
enjoys the voyage: 'deep was the pleasure I drank in with the sea-breeze;
divine the delight I drew from the heaving channel waves, from the sea-
birds on the ridges, from the white sails on their dark distance, from the
quiet, yet beclouded sky, overhanging all' (p. 117). At first it feels safe and
dream-like, but then seasickness intervenes to stop her from feeling so
comfortable. But comfort and security are relative. For her, they are not
attached to an ideal of home so much as to the process of making a
journey. Travel in literature rarely involves merely literal movements of
characters from one place to another; it is almost always to be understood
as a process of psychological development. Travel, says the **cliché**,
broadens the mind. As Lucy dreams of a future in Europe, her mind does
indeed seem to be expanding from the 'two hot, close rooms' that had
been her world in England. At the same time, though, Brontë slyly
undercuts the dream by inserting the reality of nineteenth-century sea
travel: you can dream, but you will also be sick.

In another example of sea imagery, Lucy explains why she cannot
confide her mental distress and depression to Mrs Bretton:

The difference between her and me might be figured by that between the stately ship, cruising safe on smooth seas, with its full complement of crew, a captain gay and brave, and venturous and provident; and the life-boat, which most days of the year lies dry and solitary in an old, dark boat-house, only putting to sea when the billows run high in rough weather … when danger and death between them rule the great deep. No, the 'Louisa Bretton' never was out of harbour on such a night, and in such a scene: her crew could not conceive it; so the half-drowned life-boat man keeps his own counsel, and spins no yarns. (p. 254)

Here the **metaphor** does at least two different kinds of service. It is of course a comparison between the material conditions of the two women's lives: the comforts and security enjoyed by Mrs Bretton contrasted with the dangers and uncertainties of Lucy's life. Calm sea is associated with calm minds, stormy seas with troubled ones. But the metaphor also serves to comment on the different versions of **femininity** the two women represent. Mrs Bretton, as stately as a galleon, is an attractive woman likened to a fine, seaworthy ship. Lucy is both literally and figuratively a wreck. She has just suffered a kind of nervous breakdown; she is physically enfeebled, thin and unwell – no wonder she compares herself to a boat that is always tossed about on life's storms, a boat made for danger rather than pleasure.

All the sea metaphors lead inexorably to the culmination of the novel, when Lucy is awaiting M. Paul's return from the West Indies. She, at last, is at home: he, however, is at sea. The metaphorical dangers of not having a home and not being at home, which have beset Lucy in the novel, are now **literalised** in M. Paul. Being at sea is not just an image for danger: it actually *is* dangerous and it is probable that he is killed.

Fairy tale and gothic: hunchbacks, fairies and nuns

Forget angels and hunchbacks – stick to the material world of food and drink, Madame Beck advises Lucy when she returns from her visit to Madame Walravens. But although the world of Villette is a realistically imagined place, Lucy's experiences there do not allow her to forget angels and hunchbacks. At one level, of course, *Villette* is a **realistic** novel, dealing with a version of the real world, where angels and fairies have no place. But it is also a novel saturated with references to other **genres**, particularly the **Gothic**. When Lucy is haunted by a ghostly nun, we are not really surprised to discover that there is a naturalistic explanation for the apparition. But Brontë's text in these episodes is making an explicit **allusion** to the Gothic novel of the eighteenth century, and particularly to the novels of Ann Radcliffe (1764–1823). In Radcliffe's novels an atmosphere of terror is generated around an innocent girl by a combination of unexplained incidents within a creepy environment. Castles and convents are the key settings. It is no accident that the pensionnat is a former convent; and Lucy is primed to see the nun by both her fragile emotional state and by the fact that she has heard the rumours about a nun haunting the place. It is no accident either that the nun appears when Lucy is most vulnerable – alone and already over-excited – and this seems to add to the nun's supernatural effect. Brontë's novel uses the conventions established by Radcliffe: the supernatural is simply explained away.

In addition to these Gothic manifestations, the very geography of Villette is Gothic. It is a labyrinthine place in which Lucy can get lost and be pursued by dangerous men. Being foggy, it is also somewhere difficult to know because it cannot be seen properly. It has more than its fair share of storms, which contribute to Lucy's often taut nerves. It is also a 'foreign' place, where the language and customs defeat her. It is an 'unhomely' and therefore **uncanny** site for the things that happen in Lucy's life. What is the function of this Gothic underpinning in the novel?

The Gothic novel has always been associated with women readers and women writers. The innocent heroine beset by dangers that she overcomes is a common wish-fulfilment fantasy in fiction, especially in periods when real women's lives were so circumscribed by social conventions. Brontë uses certain features of the genre because they are familiar to her readers as subtle ways of expressing some of the real problems of femininity at that time. She uses them to dramatise the difficulties (both psychological and material) of the woman who has to live and work alone in an era when women were always defined in relation to the men in their lives and were therefore deemed to be domestic creatures. As Lucy has no home, she has none of the features that go with it – including supportive men. She is unprotected both materially and psychologically. The Gothic and the uncanny go together – and in Lucy's life they are the conditions of femininity.

The fairy tale, of course, is also a genre associated with women: fairy tales are told by mothers to their children to teach them morality and obedience. *Villette* has fairy-tale elements as well as Gothic ones. Indeed, the two genres meet in the person of Madame Walravens, who is explicitly associated with the bad fairies from the stories of the Brothers Grimm. Lucy's journey through the streets of Villette, hurried along with her basket of goodies by a threatening storm, makes her look very like Little Red Riding Hood in an urban setting.

If Madame Walravens is the bad fairy of the story, then Polly Home is the good fairy, and Mrs Bretton is at least a partial realisation of the fairy godmother, bringing rescue and comfort. In contrast, though, to the story of *Jane Eyre*, where it is the plain governess who marries the (not quite) handsome prince, her boss, in this novel Lucy is not the heroine. That role is reserved for Polly, the pretty fairy child, the little princess (or countess at least). Polly's story serves to show what a woman then needed to be happy – good looks, good fortune, good sense. She is 'rewarded' for her 'virtues' and for her good luck in a sub-plot that deflects the reader's sense of *Villette* being an unremittingly gloomy book.

LANGUAGE AND STYLE

For the most part, the language of *Villette* is plain, like Lucy herself, who would pride herself on plain speaking, and who praises plain speaking in others. But if the words themselves are simple, the sentence structure very often is not. Take the following two sentences from the novel's first page, describing Graham Bretton:

> People esteemed it a grievous pity that [Mrs Bretton] had not conferred her complexion on her son, whose eyes were blue – though, even in boyhood, very piercing – and the colour of his long hair such as friends did not venture to specify, except as the sun shone on it, when they called it golden. He inherited the lines of his mother's features, however; also her good teeth, her stature (or the promise of her stature, for he was not yet full-grown), and, what was better, her health without flaw, and her spirits of that tone and quality which are better than a fortune to the possessor. (pp. 61–2)

If one sought to simplify these statements, one might just say: Graham did not have his mother's colouring because he had blue eyes and red hair, but he did have her features, teeth and figure, her health and her good nature. But Lucy's syntax is much more convoluted and less emphatic than that. Her sentences abound with qualifications ('though, even in boyhood, very piercing', 'the promise of her stature, for he was not yet full-grown'). No statement is simply made, not even the statement that he is a redhead, which is hemmed around with **periphrasis** so that the reader is left to infer his colouring.

Lucy's prose abounds with colons and semi-colons; her sentences are long and often ponderous. It is as though she is writing with exaggerated care in an attempt to be strictly accurate. In other words, the prose embodies Lucy's psychology. As a person she is careful, observant and at pains to be correct in all her behaviour and action. The same tendencies are evident in her prose. The above example is very slight, but you can easily find other moments of real syntactical contortion, especially when Lucy is being introspective and putting her powers of judgement to work on herself.

ALLUSION

Villette is saturated with **allusion**, especially to biblical stories and classic English literature. The Victorian period was, of course, a much more religious age than our own, and there was a presumption that all educated people had read their Bible. During her battle with the Church of Rome, Lucy says explicitly that she has studied the Bible for herself, so it is no surprise that she should refer to it often and use its stories to exemplify parts of her own story. As a woman who is demanding our attention across 500 pages of densely written text, Lucy uses allusion as a way of reinforcing her own authority to tell this story by situating it in a biblical context.

FRENCH

No one reading *Villette* can escape the fact that a substantial proportion of it is written in French. Lucy is not consistent in her use of French: characters who can speak only French (M. Paul and Madame Beck, for example) are often presented to us speaking in English or a strange mixture of English and French. This allows the reader to share Lucy's sense of alienation: even if we can read French, it is odd to see the two languages together, and for the non-French speaker, the unknown language can be a source of real irritation. If Lucy is not 'at home' anywhere, she makes sure that we are not 'at home' either, using language to defamiliarise and unsettle the reader.

Another reason for the use of French is to disguise the unpleasant or almost unmentionable. When such topics came up, the Victorians would say: 'Pas devant les enfants' (Not in front of the children). French lent a respectability to things that might be shocking in English, exemplified early in the novel when Lucy asks Ginevra Fanshawe what she thinks of her school.

> Oh … horrid: but I go out every Sunday, and care nothing about the *maitresses* or the *professeurs*, or the *élèves*, and send lessons *au diable*; (one daren't say that in English, you know, but it sounds quite right in French,) and thus I get on charmingly … (p. 116)

It is hard for us to reconstruct the force of Ginevra's comment as readers in the 1850s might have understood it. She is saying that she doesn't care for her teachers or fellow pupils, disguising the force of that remark by naming them in French, as if it doesn't then matter what she is saying; and she sends her lessons 'to the devil', a phrase she knows she cannot use in English (it would certainly have been regarded as shockingly profane for a young lady in 1853). French, then, is used both as a tool of estrangement and a veil of decency.

PART FOUR

TEXTUAL ANALYSIS

TEXT 1 (PAGES 95–7)

Lucy is offered a post as Miss Marchmont's companion.

'It will not be an easy life,' said she candidly, 'for I require a good deal of attention, and you will be much confined; yet, perhaps, contrasted with the existence you have lately led, it may appear tolerable.'

I reflected. Of course it ought to appear tolerable, I argued inwardly; but somehow, by some strange fatality, it would not. To live here, in this close room, the watcher of suffering, sometimes, perhaps, the butt of temper, through all that was to come of my youth; while all that was gone had passed, to say the least, not blissfully! my heart sunk one moment, then it revived; for though I forced myself to *realize* evils, I think I was too prosaic to *idealize*, and consequently to exaggerate them.

'My doubt is whether I should have strength for the undertaking,' I observed.

'This is my own scruple,' said she; 'for you look a worn-out creature!'

So I did. I saw myself in the glass, in my mourning-dress, a faded, hollow-eyed vision. Yet I thought little of the wan spectacle. The blight, I believed, was chiefly external: I still felt life at life's sources.

'What else have you in view – anything?'

'Nothing clear as yet: but I may find something.'

'So you imagine: perhaps you are right. Try your own method, then; and if it does not succeed, test mine. The chance I have offered shall be left open to you for three months.'

This was kind. I told her so, and expressed my gratitude. While I was speaking, a paroxysm of pain came on. I ministered to her; made the necessary applications, according to her directions, and, by the time she was relieved, a sort of intimacy was already formed between us. I, for my part, had learned from the manner in which she bore this attack, that she was a firm, patient woman (patient under physical pain, though sometimes perhaps excitable under long mental canker); and she, from the good-will with which I succoured her, discovered that she could influence my sympathies (such as they were). She sent for me the next day; for five or six successive days she claimed my company. Closer acquaintance, while it developed both faults and eccentricities, opened, at the same time, a view of a character I could respect. Stern and even morose as she sometimes was, I could wait on her and sit beside her with that calm which always blesses us when we are sensible that our manners, presence, contact, please and soothe the persons we serve. Even when she scolded me – which she did, now and then, very tartly – it was in such a way as did not humiliate, and left no sting; it was rather like an irascible mother rating her daughter, than a harsh mistress lecturing a dependent: lecture, indeed, she could not, though could occasionally storm. Moreover, a vein of reason ever ran through her passion: she was logical even when fierce. Ere long a growing sense of attachment began to present the thought of staying with her as companion in quite a new light; in another week I had agreed to remain.

Two hot, close rooms thus became my world; and a crippled old woman, my mistress, my friend, my all. Her service was my duty – her pain, my suffering – her relief, my hope – her anger, my punishment – her regard, my reward. I forgot that there were fields, woods, rivers, seas, an everchanging sky outside the steam-dimmed lattice of this sick-chamber; I was almost content to forget it. All within me became narrowed to my lot. Tame and still by habit, disciplined by destiny, I demanded no walks in the fresh air; my appetite needed no more than the tiny messes served for the invalid. In addition she gave me the originality of her character to study: the steadiness of her virtues, I will add, the power of her passions, to admire, the truth of her feelings to trust. All these things she had, and for these things I clung to her.

This passage occurs early in the novel, after Lucy's sojourn at Bretton, and after the 'wreck' of her previous domestic arrangements. It is our first glimpse of Lucy as a young adult rather than a child-dependant, and it focuses our attention very forcibly on the material difficulties she is to face as a middle-class woman of limited education who is thrown on to her own resources. She has no training for looking after herself, no skills to make her marketable as an employee. What, then, is she to do?

The job Miss Marchmont offers as a nurse-companion is one of very few respectable employment opportunities left open to someone of Lucy's class. (Teaching as a private governess or in a school are really the only other alternatives, and Lucy will do both later in the text.) Despite her limited options, Lucy is not attracted by this post: 'it ought to appear tolerable, I argued inwardly; but somehow, by some strange fatality, it would not'. She recognises from the outset that the job requires a very large degree of self-sacrifice. Later in the novel, when Polly offers her a similar job, Lucy rejects it, despite the potential for increased earnings, arguing that at least in her job at Madame Beck's she has a degree of freedom: 'I was not *her* [Madame Beck's] companion ... she left me free: she tied me to nothing – not to herself – not even to her interests' (p. 383). The seeds of the later rejection are sown in the earlier experience at Miss Marchmont's, where Lucy's autonomy is undermined by her mistress's complete dependence. One of the functions of this interlude is that it helps to explain choices Lucy will make later; it is a very short period in her life, but it is formative of her character.

Miss Marchmont herself is both a tragic and quasi-tyrannical figure. We later learn the story of her lost love – a story that more properly belongs in **romantic fiction**. Lucy's focus, though, is on the *results* of Miss Marchmont's loss. The figure of the invalid is often heroic in Victorian fiction, and the female invalid in particular is supposed to be touchingly beautiful and admirably patient. The representation of Miss Marchmont is much more realistic. She is not young and pretty; she lives with constant pain which, far from drawing out her best qualities, makes her often bad-tempered and caustic; she is not easy to live with. Lucy can admire her mistress's sterling qualities, 'the steadiness of her virtues ... the power of her passions ... the truth of her feelings', but that does not make the situation ideal. Their relationship is one of enforced and constant intimacy, and that can often be uncomfortable. When M. Paul later criticises Lucy for her failings, he takes the nun who nurses those with terrible illnesses as his example of feminine perfection (p. 279). He calls her an egotist for her inability to set aside her personal disinclination to do her duty. Lucy knows better.

She knows, however, that there are dangers in self-abnegation. Much of the novel is about her quest for an identity of her own – an identity that she forges through her work and relationships, but which finally comes from her inner self. In the final paragraph of the extract she suggests that in nursing Miss Marchmont she had virtually lost her sense of self. The old woman had become her 'all'; her own desires and nature had been utterly repressed to the needs of the invalid: 'Her service was my duty – her pain, my suffering – her relief, my hope – her anger, my punishment – her regard, my reward.' This is problematic for Lucy's identity as an individual. In serving the old lady, she becomes more like her, living her own life in terms of the other woman's needs. This was a common view of how women should live their lives in the nineteenth century: femininity, it was believed, was best expressed in serving husbands, parents, children or, more widely, the poor and the sick. Lucy is seduced into taking this role and putting aside her own needs by the job's apparent safety. Accepting the home and material security offered by Miss Marchmont despite the restrictions is useful discipline for her future· life in Villette. She learns that she requires freedom and opportunity to exercise her talents, so later – even in the community of the school – she chooses solitude rather than intimacy with others. When she works for Miss Marchmont, she purchases material safety at the price of psychological security.

Finally, although we learn much about the relatively minor character Miss Marchmont, we learn most of it through Lucy's eyes. Miss Marchmont is *described* because it is her effects on Lucy that count, not the woman herself. In describing Miss Marchmont, Lucy describes her own preferences – and thus, in a typically indirect way, describes herself.

TEXT *2*   (PAGES 392–4)

Ginevra and Lucy discuss Lucy's character, origins and status as they prepare to go out for the evening together.

As Miss Fanshawe and I were dressing in the dormitory of the Rue Fossette, she (Miss F.) suddenly burst into a laugh.

'What now?' I asked; for she had suspended the operation of arranging her attire, and was gazing at me.

'It seems so odd,' she replied, with her usual half-honest, half-insolent unreserve, 'that you and I should now be so much on a level, visiting in the same sphere; having the same connections.'

'Why yes,' said I; 'I had not much respect for the connections you chiefly frequented awhile ago: Mrs Cholmondeley and Co. would never have suited me at all.'

'Who *are* you, Miss Snowe?' she inquired, in a tone of such undisguised and unsophisticated curiosity, as made me laugh in my turn.

'You used to call yourself a nursery-governess; when you first came here you really had the care of the children in this house: I have seen you carry little Georgette in your arms, like a bonne – few governesses would have condescended so far – and now Madame Beck treats you with more courtesy than she treats the Parisienne, St. Pierre; and that proud chit, my cousin, makes you her bosom friend!'

'Wonderful!' I agreed, much amused at her mystification. 'Who am I indeed? Perhaps a personage in disguise. Pity I don't look the character.'

'I wonder you are not more flattered by all this,' she went on: 'you take it with strange composure. If you really are the nobody I once thought you, you must be a cool hand.'

'The nobody you once thought me!' I repeated, and my face grew a little hot; but I would not be angry: of what importance was a school-girl's crude use of the terms nobody and somebody? I confined myself, therefore, to the remark that I had merely met with civility; and asked 'what she saw in civility to throw the recipient into a fever of confusion?'

'One can't help wondering at some things,' she persisted.

'Wondering at marvels of your own manufacture. Are you ready at last?'

'Yes; let me take your arm.'

'I would rather not: we will walk side by side.'

When she took my arm, she always leaned upon me her whole weight; and, as I was not a gentleman, or her lover, I did not like it.

'There, again!' she cried. 'I thought, by offering to take your arm, to intimate approbation of your dress and general appearance: I meant it as a compliment.'

'You did? You meant, in short, to express that you are not ashamed to be seen in the street with me? That if Mrs Cholmondeley should be fondling her lap-dog at some window, or Colonel de Hamal picking his teeth in a balcony, and should catch a glimpse of us, you would not quite blush for your companion?'

'Yes,' she said, with that directness which was her best point – which gave an honest plainness to her very fibs when she told them – which was, in short, the salt, the sole preservative ingredient of a character otherwise not formed to keep.

I delegated the trouble of commenting on this 'yes' to my countenance; or rather, my under-lip voluntarily anticipated my tongue: of course, reverence and solemnity were not the feelings expressed in the look I gave her.

'Scornful, sneering creature!' she went on, as we crossed a great square and entered the quiet, pleasant park, our nearest way to the Rue Crécy. 'Nobody in this world was ever such a Turk to me as you are!'

'You bring it on yourself: let me alone: have the sense to be quiet: I will let you alone.'

'As if one *could* let you alone, when you are so peculiar and mysterious!'

'The mystery and peculiarity being entirely the conception of your own brain – maggots – neither more nor less, be so good as to keep them out of my sight.'

'But *are* you anybody?' persevered she, pushing her hand, in spite of me, under my arm; and that arm pressed itself with inhospitable closeness against my side, by way of keeping out the intruder.

'Yes,' I said, 'I am a rising character: once an old lady's companion, then a nursery-governess, now a school-teacher.'

For the most part, Lucy appears a very solemn, even humourless, character, but occasionally there are flashes of wit and raillery, which the above passage exemplifies. Lucy and Ginevra are preparing to go out with the Bassompierres, an evening that is to be filled with the great and the good of Villette. It is a mark of the social progress that Lucy has made since her anonymous arrival some months earlier.

The relationship between Lucy and Ginevra is based on the attraction of opposites. Lucy is introspective and quiet; Ginevra is outgoing, showy and loud. The conversation they have in this instance reintroduces one of the major themes of *Villette* as a whole – the question of identity and what it is based on, though the importance of the theme is partially disguised by the bantering tone of the conversation. Ginevra is amazed that someone like Lucy could possibly share her own social milieu. Lucy's riposte – 'I had not much respect for the connections you chiefly frequented awhile ago: Mrs Cholmondeley and Co. would never have suited me at all' – is an attack on Ginevra's presumption of social superiority. Lucy is saying that she would not have wanted to go to parties with Mrs Cholmondeley, even if she had been invited; to mix with such people is not her aspiration. Ginevra, obtuse as ever, probably does not recognise the force of Lucy's comment. Nonetheless, when she asks who Lucy really is, even though she does so with mere 'undisguised and unsophisticated curiosity', she begins a conversation that goes to the heart of *Villette*.

For Ginevra, identity is bound up with appearance (especially clothes and jewels) and social relationships. A person is his/her outward looks combined with his/her standing in the material and social world. Like many other characters in the novel, she is prone to judge by appearance alone, hence her tone of wonder that the plain and friendless Lucy has risen so far. In an earlier conversation, she had asked Lucy what she would give to be Ginevra, and she had ruthlessly compared and contrasted their very different fortunes. In that earlier conversation Ginevra had presumed that all the advantages were on her side: she is well-born, if poor, young, pretty, accomplished (though not learned), and certainly attractive to men. As for Lucy:

> I suppose you are nobody's daughter, since you took care of little children when you first came to Villette: you have no relations; you can't call yourself young at twenty-three; you have no attractive accomplishments – no beauty. As to admirers, you hardly know what they are. (p. 215)

In fact, in both examples, Ginevra presumes that identity is bound up with extrinsic attributes; it has nothing to do with the internal qualities or the inner life. Without those external things, Lucy is a 'nobody'.

Being called a nobody hurts Lucy, but less so than being described by Dr John as an 'inoffensive shadow' (p. 403) because she cares less for Ginevra's good opinion. But even in this extract it brings home to her how much she is judged by things that she would like to believe do not matter. Just after this extract, Lucy comments on the narrowness of Ginevra's conceptions of selfhood as the younger girl speculates on who Lucy really is: 'she rang the most fanciful changes on this theme; proving ... her incapacity to conceive how any person not bolstered up by birth or wealth, not supported by some consciousness of name or connection, could maintain an attitude of reasonable dignity' (p. 394).

The need to attack Ginevra marks the extent of Lucy's pain. With Ginevra's careless remark the tone of the conversation alters, though Ginevra does not realise that she has upset Lucy. From the moment of being described as a nobody Lucy becomes angry. She is less willing to banter, and is more on her dignity, asserting through her words and actions that she has a self to be reckoned with. She becomes more caustic with the younger girl; she refuses her arm, expresses her scorn by pulling a face, demands to be left alone as they walk through the park, and describes Ginevra's brain as rotten (maggotty). Paradoxically, this serves only to make Ginevra more fascinated and intrigued. The clue is in her remark that nobody is 'such a Turk to me as you are'. In other words, nobody ever takes the trouble to correct Ginevra's faults, to speak to her truthfully, or to attack her preconceptions. Lucy pays Ginevra the compliment of taking her seriously. This makes Lucy extremely unusual and fascinating in Ginevra's eyes, leading her to demand: 'But *are* you anybody?'

Lucy's answers to questions about her identity are very instructive. In the passage she gives two answers: she describes herself as 'a personage in disguise' and 'a rising character', supplementing the latter answer with her professional CV to date – 'once an old lady's companion, then a nursery-governess, now a school-teacher'. Both these answers point to fiction as one of the places from which identity is learned: a 'personage in disguise', after all, is a character from a **romance**, whereas 'character' is the word used to describe people in stories. Neither answer, though, positively identifies the attributes of Lucy Snowe. The figure in disguise refuses disclosure and, in any case, Lucy does not 'look the part', as she admits herself; the list of jobs she has done merely reiterates the version of selfhood that Ginevra understands – a self is dependent on its social/professional standing. At different points in the novel Lucy is a kind of figure in disguise. After her success in the school play, when she has momentarily enjoyed displaying her talents and being the centre of attention, she returns immediately to the shadows:

> I had acted enough for one evening; it was time I retired into myself and my ordinary life. My dun-coloured dress … would not suit a waltz or a quadrille. Withdrawing to a quiet nook, whence unobserved I could observe – the ball, its splendours and its pleasures passed before me as spectacle. (p. 211)

Even her dress – 'dun-coloured', meaning grey-brown or mousy – is camouflage. No wonder, then, that Dr John sees her as an inoffensive shadow. But being called a nobody hurts, whatever her temperamental preference for disguise. For despite her appearance and manner, one of the things that *Villette* argues very forcibly is that even quiet people live with passion, can suffer and love with real intensity, can be 'somebodies' within their own parameters.

TEXT 3 (PAGES 480–2)

Lucy meets Madame Walravens.

The room was large, and had a fine old ceiling, and almost church-like windows of coloured glass; but it was desolate, and in the shadow of the coming storm, looked strangely lowering. Within – opened a smaller room; there, however, the blind of the single casement was closed; through the deep gloom few details of furniture were apparent. These few I amused myself by puzzling to make out; and, in particular, I was attracted by the outline of a picture on the wall.

By-and-bye the picture seemed to give way: to my bewilderment, it shook, sunk, it rolled back into nothing; its vanishing left an opening arched, leading into an arched passage, with a mystic, winding stair; both passage and stair were of cold stone, uncarpeted and unpainted. Down this donjon stair descended a tap, tap, like a stick; soon, there fell on the steps a shadow, and last of all, I was aware of a substance.

Yet, was it actual substance, this appearance approaching me? this obstruction, partially darkening the arch?

It drew near, and I saw it well. I began to comprehend where I was. Well might this old square be named quarter of the Magii – well might the three towers overlooking it, own for godfathers three mystic sages of a dead and dark art. Hoar enchantment here prevailed; a spell had opened for elf-land – that cell-like room, that vanishing picture, that arch and passage, and stair stone, were all parts of a fairy tale. Distincter even than these scenic details stood the chief figure – Cunegonde, the sorceress! Malevola, the evil fairy. How was she?

She might have been three feet high, but she had no shape; her skinny hands rested upon each other, and pressed the gold knob of a wand-like ivory staff. Her face was large, set, not upon her shoulders, but before her breast; she seemed to have no neck; I should have said there were a hundred years in her features, and more perhaps in her eyes – her malign, unfriendly eyes, with thick gray brows above, and livid lids all round. How severely they viewed me, with a sort of dull displeasure.

This being wore a gown of brocade, dyed bright blue, full-tinted as the gentianella flower, and covered with satin foliage in a large pattern; over the gown a costly shawl, gorgeously bordered, and so large for her, that its many-coloured fringe swept the floor. But her chief points were her jewels; she had long, clear ear-rings, blazing with a lustre which could not be borrowed or false; she had rings on her skeleton hands, with thick gold hoops, and stones – purple, green, and blood-red. Hunchbacked, dwarfish, and doting, she was adorned like a barbarian queen.

'Que me voulez-vous?' she said hoarsely, with the voice of male rather than female old age; and, indeed, a silver beard bristled her chin.

I delivered my basket and my message.

'Is that all?' she demanded.

'It is all,' said I.

'Truly, it was well worth while,' she answered. 'Return to Madame Beck, and tell her I can buy fruit when I want it, et quant à ses félicitations, je m'en moque!' And this courteous dame turned her back.

Just as she turned, a peal of thunder broke, and a flash of lightning blazed broad over salon and boudoir. The tale of magic seemed to proceed with due accompaniment of the elements. The wanderer, decoyed into the enchanted castle, heard rising, outside, the spell-wakened tempest.

Lucy's visit to Madame Walravens is a set piece of fairy tale and **Gothic** conventions. Although we do not know it at first, it is part of the plot to separate Lucy from M. Paul. The atmosphere of intrigue which thus surrounds the episode adds to its Gothic feel. Madame Beck has asked Lucy to deliver a basket of birthday fruit to the Rue des Mages. The purpose of the visit is to tell her M. Paul's story and show her his financial commitments so that she will not be tempted to try to marry him. The plot misfires because the very fact of its having being constructed alerts Lucy to the possibility that M. Paul really feels something for her.

Lucy approaches the Rue des Mages as a storm is brewing. When she enters the house, the storm and the 'church-like windows of coloured glass' combine to create the conventional atmosphere and décor of

Gothic fiction. The room is dark, making it difficult for Lucy to interpret what she sees. For example, the picture at the far end of the room actually conceals a door, so Lucy is unnerved when it suddenly opens. The tension is built up by the gradual unfolding of events. There is the disembodied sound of a stick tapping in the distance, then there is a shadow thrown through the opening. But even when the owner of both becomes visible, the mystery is not complete; Madame Walravens is so unlike a normal human being that Lucy finds it difficult to interpret what she sees. The narrative draws on the convention that mystery is frightening, and heightens the effect by presenting a real figure who appears to belong to fairy tale.

In fairy tales it is usual to judge by appearance: pretty girls and handsome princes are good, ugly old women are bad. The novel has prepared us to question this mode of judgement, but on this occasion the old woman is ugly both inside and out. Lucy's first impression is augmented when she later hears how Madame Walravens destroyed the love affair between M. Paul and Justine-Marie. In the passage, though, the first impression is very strong on its own. This dwarf woman, whose head appears to grow from her chest, is both monstrous and grotesque. Her physical deformation is mirrored in her attitude and reinforced by 'her malign, unfriendly eyes ... How severely they viewed me, with a sort of dull displeasure'. In addition, Madame Walravens is extravagantly and inappropriately dressed. The rich patterns of her dress and shawl necessarily draw attention to the misshapen body beneath. Her hands, covered with costly jewels, are those of a skeleton. She is an **uncanny** figure, who combines the living and the dead in one body. In her last comment on the woman's physique, Lucy says she was: 'Hunchbacked, dwarfish, and doting, she was adorned like a barbarian queen.' It is an image of perverted power (a barbarian queen should be magnificent, not horrible) and of misplaced finery: the elaborate jewels and clothes do not belong with that body.

Miss Marchmont, Lucy's first mistress, also had a stricken, misshapen body, but there is a world of difference between the two women. The first woman offered employment – a safety of sorts. The second appears demonically powerful and threatening, an impression exaggerated by the accident of stormy weather, which Lucy sees as Madame Walravens's 'due accompaniment'. For a moment she fantasises that she herself is a fairy-tale figure, 'decoyed into the enchanted castle' listening to a storm brought about by a spell. The truth is more prosaic – there has been a plot but no magic.

What, then, is the function of these effects? The Gothic is a literature of danger, but not of the supernatural variety. There is to be a battle for both her heart (will she be allowed to love M. Paul?) and her soul (will she convert to Catholicism?). The Gothic atmosphere pervading this scene expresses not physical danger for Lucy, but psychological pressure. It is a way of externalising the conflict in Lucy's head. *Villette* is not a novel of action. Most of its 'events' might more properly be called feelings or emotions, for most of its struggles and conflicts are internal. The story of an inner life needs externalised correlations to help the reader to follow the plot and its resolutions. This scene in the Rue des Mages is one such example of externalising mental conflict in the novel.

PART FIVE

BACKGROUND

CHARLOTTE BRONTË AND HER LIFE

Born in 1816 in Thornton, Yorkshire, Charlotte Brontë was brought up in Haworth, where her father was the clergyman. She was the third of six children born to Patrick Brontë, a taciturn Northern Irishman who had dragged himself up from peasant origins to become an ordained priest, and Maria (née Branwell), who died when Charlotte was only four years old. The other children were Maria (b. 1813), Elizabeth (b. 1815), Branwell (b. 1817), Emily (b. 1818) and Anne (b. 1820). The last two sisters also became novelists.

Charlotte was educated partly at home and partly at the Clergy Daughters' School at Cowan Bridge, where the harsh regime contributed to the deaths of her two elder sisters in 1825. Charlotte and her younger sister Emily were removed from the school and then more or less educated themselves with the aid of their father's library. They were cared for by their aunt Elizabeth Branwell, who had come to live with them after Mrs Brontë's death.

The Brontë family were socially isolated at Haworth, so the remaining four children were very much together and lived an intense fantasy life. Charlotte teamed up with Branwell to write epic narratives of an imaginary land in Africa named Angria, while the two other sisters worked together on the Gondal saga. These fictions were extravagant, passionate and romantic, and informed the later work of the three surviving sisters.

The end of childhood brought the need to earn a living, and, given their class, the girls had no option but to become governesses. They were all miserable in this occupation and looked around for alternatives. With money from their aunt, Charlotte and Emily went to Brussels in 1842 and enrolled at a boarding-school run by Constantin Heger in order to learn languages so that they could eventually run their own school from the parsonage. The stay in Brussels was enormously significant for Charlotte. She developed an impossible attachment to M. Heger (who was married), and the desolation she felt at the rejection of her love is part of the background of *Villette*. Brussels itself became the model for Villette, Madame Beck is alleged to resemble Madame Heger, and M. Paul is a partial portrait of Heger himself. The plan for the Brontës' school was eventually thwarted by lack of capital to fund it.

Charlotte had been writing for the whole of her adult life, sometimes with her brother, but increasingly on her own. She had ambitions to write for profit, and in 1836 sent her poems to the poet laureate, Robert Southey, asking for advice. Southey replied many months later: 'Literature cannot be the business of a woman's life, and it ought not to be. The more she is engaged in her proper duties, the less leisure she will have for it, even as an accomplishment and a recreation' (Lyndall Gordon, *Charlotte Brontë: A Passionate Life*, 1994, p. 64). In Southey's opinion, women should stick to marriage and motherhood as their careers. He had nothing to say to a woman who had to earn her living and who had no one to marry. Her response to this view of feminine 'business' can be found in all her novels. None the less, it was not until 1845 that she began seriously to consider the possibility of publication. She found some of Emily's poems in a drawer and was struck by their power. With the promise of anonymity, she persuaded both her sisters to put their poems with hers in a volume entitled *Poems by Currer, Ellis and Acton Bell* (1846). They used pseudonyms because they knew that women's poetry was likely to be misjudged – literature cannot be 'woman's business'. They paid for the publication themselves and sold exactly six copies.

Undaunted, all three sisters completed novels in 1846 and sent out the manuscripts to various publishers. They received little encouragement, but when Charlotte's book, *The Professor*, eventually received an encouraging notice from a publisher, she was inspired to complete her second novel, *Jane Eyre*, and send it to Smith, Elder and Co. The publisher loved it and brought it out in October 1847. The success it enjoyed helped Emily and Anne to find publishers for *Wuthering Heights* and *Agnes Grey*, which were published two months later.

Jane Eyre was an immediate sensation, provoking everything from the sincerest praise to the most hostile criticism. Charlotte, though, was distracted by family troubles. Branwell, incapacitated by alcoholism, died in September 1848. Two months later Emily died from tuberculosis, and

Anne followed her in July 1849. Charlotte, the sole survivor, was left to cope with her father, who was going blind and becoming increasingly difficult. None the less, she published a second novel, *Shirley*, in 1849, and *Villette*, her last book, came out in 1853. Before she died, she enjoyed a certain celebrity status, meeting most of the major novelists of the day, and she found personal happiness when she married her father's curate, Arthur Bell Nicholls, in 1854. She died a few months later, in March 1855, from symptoms related to pregnancy, having shown that Southey was wrong, and that literature could indeed be a woman's business.

BRONTË'S WRITING

Charlotte's first completed novel was called *The Professor* and it was not published until after her death (1857). Like *Villette*, it draws on her experiences in Brussels, but this time the main protagonist is a young man. William Crimsworth is an orphan who has tried to make his way by working in trade, but has failed and feels excluded. He seeks his fortune in Brussels, where he obtains a post as an English teacher. There he falls in love with a pupil-teacher, Frances Henri, but he is pursued by the machiavellian headmistress, Madame Reuter. He resists her blandishments, eventually moving to a better post and happily marrying Frances. The themes of the novel are similar to those in *Villette*: the conflict between duty and passion, the need for love, and the necessity of social respectability and a 'place' in the world.

Of the works that Brontë published in her lifetime, *Jane Eyre* (1847) is the most strictly comparable to *Villette*. It, too, is a first-person narrative – **autobiographical fiction**, with elements of *Bildungsroman*, the **Gothic** and the fairy tale about it. Like Lucy, Jane is an orphan. She does not fit in with the relatives who look after her, and she is sent away to school. The regime there is harsh, but she takes from her education sufficient knowledge to earn her living as a governess. She finds a post at Thornfield House, home of Mr Rochester, and it becomes clear that the two are falling in love. Unknown to Jane, there is an impediment to their relationship in the shape of Mr Rochester's first wife, a madwoman confined to the attic. After an aborted wedding ceremony (Rochester intends bigamously to marry Jane), she leaves him and wanders destitute through the countryside, before ending up with a family who turn out to be her cousins. She works in the village school for a while, but is released from this and her cousin's persistent proposals of marriage by a legacy from a distant uncle. She decides to go back to Rochester, and finds him a widower, maimed in a fire in which his mad wife has been killed. They marry and live happily ever after.

Like Lucy (and, indeed, Crimsworth), Jane is a displaced person, with no social standing of her own. But also like Lucy, Jane is very assertive of her rights to happiness and love as prerequisites for a fully rounded life.

Shirley (1849) is rather different. Although it too considers the position of women, it is set around the 1810s and deals with social problems arising from the Industrial Revolution. Two love stories take place against the backdrop of the Luddite riots, when workers rebelled against the introduction of machinery that was to take away their employment. Shirley Keeldar, one of the heroines, is a wealthy heiress with a mind of her own. The other heroine, Caroline Helstone, is more shy and retiring, has no money and suffers a persistent sense of not belonging. The two men with whom the women fall in love are brothers. Robert Gerard is an industrialist, one of those introducing the machines despite the opposition of his workforce. He is often insensitive, almost ruined financially by his forward-looking machine policy, and is nearly killed in a riot. Believing that Shirley loves him, and partly motivated by her money, he proposes to her. Shirley, though, is in love with his more sensitive brother, Louis, and she rejects Robert's advances. Meanwhile, Caroline is pining for Robert and wasting away. Eventually the couples are appropriately sorted out and all is well.

What connects *Shirley* to Brontë's other novels is the figure of Caroline Helstone – a woman who is not allowed a purpose or social place of her own. She lives with her uncle in enforced idleness, forbidden even to consider the career of governess, and her purposeless existence makes her prey to depression. Shirley, more fortunately placed in terms of wealth, is able to show that a woman's 'business' can indeed be business as well as love and marriage. Caroline, without love, is a desperate creature who has nothing to live for until Robert comes to his senses. Against a background of social upheaval, Brontë shows an inner world of hopeless passion and psychological desperation – these are her real and repeated themes.

HISTORICAL AND LITERARY BACKGROUND

It would be only too easy to assume that a novel focusing so closely on the individual mind is unconcerned with social or political history. But even if, as Tony Tanner puts it in his introduction, Lucy Snowe is a 'self without society', that does not mean that her problems are purely local or individual. It is perfectly clear, for example, that in Lucy's crisis of conscience over the relative merits of Catholicism and Protestantism, Brontë was responding to urgent contemporary debates about religion in England (see Part 3, pp. 68–9). Above all, though, her writings consistently exhibit a concern with what came to be known as 'The Woman Question'.

The Woman Question concerned society's attitudes to middle- and upper-class women – or 'ladies', as they were then styled. (Working-class women were viewed almost as a separate species and were dealt with very differently.) Mid-Victorian England presumed that ladies were passive, weak, incapable of sustained intellectual engagement, and made solely for the purposes of marriage and motherhood. They would not need to work since fathers and husbands would provide for them; consequently, they did not need to be well educated. Indeed, a lady's education fitted her for little else than being a decorative accessory to her husband's home. She might paint watercolours, play a little music, engage in conversation, but she was not expected to do much more. But what about those women who could not marry? Or as writer Frances Power Cobbe (1822–1904) was to put it in the title of an article just ten years after *Villette* was published, 'What shall we do with our old maids?' (*Frazer's Magazine*, November 1862). The 'problem' of unmarriageable women was becoming urgent by the mid-century, when there was clearly an imbalance between the numbers of adult men and women. If many women could not marry and rely on a husband's support, what could they do?

With poor education, and certainly no access to the highly paid professions, the only respectable careers open to them were in governessing, schoolteaching, or work as paid companions. These jobs were badly paid and involved a compromise in social status – a 'real lady' should not have to work. The cultural belief that this problem was urgent and acute is witnessed by the number of Victorian novels that centre on such women: alongside *Jane Eyre* and Lucy Snowe in *Villette*, there is Anne Brontë's pathetic *Agnes Grey* (1848), William Thackeray's wicked if attractive Becky Sharpe in *Vanity Fair* (1847–8), Mary Elizabeth Braddon's dangerously pretty governess in *Lady Audley's Secret* (1862), George Eliot's eminently sensible Mary Garth in *Middlemarch* (1871–2), and Henry James's neurotic and ambiguous heroine in *The Turn of the Screw* (1898), to name just the most famous examples.

The eponymous heroine of *Jane Eyre* comments:

> Women are supposed to be very calm generally; but women feel just as men feel; they need exercise for their faculties, and a field for their efforts as much as their brothers do; they suffer from too rigid a restraint, too absolute a stagnation, precisely as men would suffer; and it is narrow-minded in their more privileged fellow-creatures to say that they ought to confine themselves to making puddings and knitting stockings, to playing on the piano and embroidering bags. It is thoughtless to condemn them, or laugh at them, if they seek to do more or learn more than custom has pronounced necessary for their sex. (Chapter 12)

This is a very precise expression too of Lucy's problems. Love and a field of action are what she requires, and these are precisely what her situation denies her. Convention dictates that she should be self-effacing and calm; that she should repress her feelings and be satisfied with her lot. But such a life is a living death, Lucy suggests, when she recalls her passion for Dr John and the severity with which she has repressed it: 'I thought the tomb unquiet, and dreamed strangely of disturbed earth, and of hair, still golden and living, obtruded through coffin-chinks' (p. 451). The striking and macabre image of a woman buried alive expresses metaphorically and individually the larger social problem of The Woman Question.

PART SIX

CRITICAL HISTORY & BROADER PERSPECTIVES

RECEPTION AND EARLY CRITICAL VIEWS

Currer Bell's new novel was eagerly awaited by reviewers who had enjoyed *Jane Eyre* but been disappointed in *Shirley*. While *Villette* was praised, the reviewers had their doubts about what the novel was seeking to do, and even about its status as a novel. For example, the reviewer for the *Eclectic Review* (March 1853) argued that it was a novel without a proper regard for plot.

> The plot itself lacks incident, it contains few of what the dramatists call *situations*, and it is chiefly transacted in a girls' boarding school. Hence the work mostly consists of dialogue, and … it tires by its sameness. The greatest master of fiction that ever wrote would have fatigued his readers if he had dwelt upon crochet, guard-chains, cookery, and dress, and all the vapid details of a girls' school-room. (Quoted in Miriam Allott (ed.), *Jane Eyre and Villette: A Collection of Critical Essays*, p. 92)

These comments actually say more about the critic's expectations of fiction than they do about what actually happens in *Villette*. (A novel full of dialogue? A novel all about crochet and cookery?) Anne Mozley, writing in the *Christian Remembrancer* (April 1853), argues that the novel's plot suffered from a 'want of continuity', and that it behaved more like the random autobiography than the structured novel (Allott, op. cit., p. 107). She suggested, for example, that the Miss Marchmont episode had no function in the story and was simply a random incident in the heroine's life. Similarly, the *Spectator*'s reviewer (February 1853) also argued that the novel had no plot, though he still thought it worth reading:

> Of plot, strictly taken as a series of coherent events all leading to a common result, there is none; no more, at least, than there would be in two years of any person's life who had occupations and acquaintances, and told us about them. Of interesting scenes, and of well-drawn characters there is, on the other hand, abundance; and these, though they fail to stimulate the curiosity of the reader like

a well-constructed plot, sustain the attention, and keep up a pleasant emotion, from the first page to the last. (Ibid., p. 81)

From these comments it is easy to see that reviewers had quite strict opinions about the nature of prose fiction: they presumed that it would deal with external incident rather than inner life, and that structure and progression were central to good fiction.

Where nineteenth-century critics differ most from present-day readers is in the importance they attached to characters such as Polly and Dr John. The representation of Polly as a little girl – which readers nowadays might well find sentimental and unrealistic – was singled out for praise by many reviewers. Polly so impressed the reviewer for the *Athenaeum* (February 1853) that he was disappointed by her sudden disappearance from the book, having assumed that her story would be central: 'we hoped that Currer Bell was going to trace out the girlhood, courtship, and matrimony of such a curious, elvish mite,' he wrote (ibid., p. 86). For the reviewer in *Putnam's Monthly Magazine* (May 1853), she was 'the "creation" of the book', original and brilliant (ibid., p. 97).

The other key area of disagreement between critics then and now is over the twinned issues of morality and propriety. For Victorian readers, one of the purposes of fiction was to paint an explicit moral, and the excuse for reading novels was that they improved behaviour. In the service of moral improvement they were supposed to be bastions of respectability and propriety. The critic George Henry Lewes – a great fan of Charlotte Brontë – pointed out that these features could not be found in *Villette* (or in *Jane Eyre* with which he compared it). In the *Leader* (February 1853) he wrote that Currer Bell's heroes and heroines 'are men and women of deep feeling, clear intellects, vehement tempers, bad manners, ungraceful, yet loveable persons' (Allott, op. cit., p. 80). He railed against the purely conventional and proper hero and heroine and praised *Villette* as an '*original book*. Every page, every paragraph is sharp with *individuality*' (ibid., p. 81). That individuality and lack of respect for convention made other reviewers queasy. In particular, Lucy's demand for love as a necessary right caused unease. The review in the *Dublin Magazine* (November 1853) disapproved of *Villette*'s moral: 'that there can be no real happiness to a woman … independently of the exercise of those affections with which nature has endowed her' (ibid., p. 100). And

Harriet Martineau wrote at greater length on the same theme in the *Daily News* (February 1853). She argued that *Villette* was a painful book because of the prevalence of unrequited love as its theme:

> All the female characters, in all their thoughts and lives, are full of one thing ...
> love. It begins with the child of six years old, at the opening – a charming picture –
> and it closes with it at the last page; and so dominant is this idea – so incessant is
> the writer's tendency to describe the need of being loved ... (Allott, op. cit., p. 76)

Martineau found this a dangerous tendency in the novel. There is more to a woman's life, she argued, than love, and even non-prudish readers would turn away from the constant harping on the theme of passion.

In short, the reviewers discovered the story of Lucy Snowe to be unconventional: the novel is not conventional in its structure, it is not populated by conventional characters, and it harbours unconventional (even improper) feelings. For some, these attributes were the source of the novel's power: for others, they were disquieting. The most famous and enduring response to the novel is, ironically, not from a published review, but expressed in a private letter to a friend from poet and critic Matthew Arnold in April 1843:

> Why is *Villette* disagreeable? Because the writer's mind contains nothing but
> hunger, rebellion and rage, and therefore that is all that she can, in fact, put into
> her book. No fine writing can hide this thoroughly, and it will be fatal to her in
> the long run. (Allott, op. cit., p. 93)

His remarks are at least as much a critique of what he perceives to be Charlotte Brontë's character as they are of the book. However, judging the quality of a work by the perceived character of the writer, or vice versa, was a typical Victorian critical method.

CRITICAL HISTORY

In the years after Charlotte Brontë's death the same **ambiguous** responses to her work continued, though with one significant addition. In 1853, although anyone curious enough could have discovered that Currer Bell was a Yorkshire parson's daughter, there was little information about her life. This changed in 1857 with the publication of

Elizabeth Gaskell's *Life of Charlotte Brontë*, after which studies of her novels took a biographical turn. The desire to find links between her fiction and her life is understandable, given that her two most famous novels are **autobiographical fictions** and draw heavily on her own experiences. Thus John Skelton, reviewing Mrs Gaskell's *Life* in the *National Review* in 1857, regarded *Villette* as 'an elaborate psychological examination' and praises its power; but he also excuses what he sees as some of Brontë's faults by reference to her life:

> as we recall the lone woman sitting by the desolate hearthstone, and remember all that she lost and suffered, we cannot blame very gravely the occasional harshness and impatience of her language when dealing with men who have been cast in a different mode. (Allott, op. cit., p. 127)

And for Émile Montégut in the *Revue des deux mondes*, also in 1857, 'The life of Charlotte Brontë is the very substance of her novels' (ibid., p. 133).

Just as in the original reviews of *Villette*, she had both her supporters and detractors, especially in relation to her delineation of character. The novelist Margaret Oliphant (1828–97) was impressed by Brontë's power, but distressed by the host of pale imitations that she felt had been spawned by *Jane Eyre* and *Villette*. The poet Algernon Charles Swinburne (1837–1909) was full of praise for Brontë's characters (see Allott, pp. 144–8), but the critic Leslie Stephen regarded them merely as the creations of an earnest young woman rather than a genius (ibid., pp. 148–56). On the whole, though, there was agreement that Brontë had achieved lasting fame, and the debate raged rather around whether that fame should rest on the achievement of *Jane Eyre* or *Villette*.

In the early twentieth century, slightly different – if related – principles of criticism came into play. In his influential book *Early Victorian Novelists* (1934, quoted in Allott, op. cit.), Lord David Cecil judged Brontë's works as narrow and merely subjective, taking social commentary and wider political action as paradigms of what good fiction should cover. He criticised *Villette* for its lack of artistic coherence and unity, focusing on the novel's changing points of interest (from Polly, to Lucy and Dr John, to Polly and Dr John, to Lucy and M. Paul) as evidence of the rambling plot. In other words, he judged Brontë's novel by the standards of a very different kind of fiction, a fiction of externalised incident, and his judgement had a long reach, relegating

Villette to a definite second place behind *Jane Eyre*. Fashions in criticism change, however, and in 1958 Robert Heilman's *From Jane Austen to Joseph Conrad* (quoted in Allott, op. cit.) suggested that the works should be measured against the **Gothic** tradition rather than the **realist** one. He suggested that she both used and subverted the traditions of Gothic fiction for the purposes of psychological drama, humour and demonstrating Lucy Snowe's maturing personality in action. He argues that her technique is both brilliant and innovative. The opposing views of Cecil and Heilman about the role of fiction – social versus psychological – do not allow the same novel to be judged positively. There are, however, other methods of criticism that do not rely on attributing a particular purpose to a certain type of writing, and then deciding whether the text in question lives up to it or not.

  More recently *Villette* has produced some brilliant readings that draw on contemporary models of literary theory. These models do not 'judge' a work so much as attempt to analyse how it 'works'. The fortunes of *Villette* have certainly been improved by this shift, and the prevalence of **feminist** literary theory in particular has renewed interest in Brontë's last novel.

Recent criticism

Marxist approaches

One of the key problems with Brontë studies generally is the overwhelming tendency to use a simplistic biographical approach to 'explain' the works. Marxist literary theories, although they consider biography, are also open to the possibility that wider social and political issues may affect the author. One of the myths clinging to the Brontës is that their works were written by solitary geniuses who had no points of contact with the external world.

  The classic Marxist study of all three sisters is Terry Eagleton's *Myths of Power: A Marxist Study of the Brontës* (1975). In his introduction, he argues that all novels are in some sense political, and criticism should aim to explain the relationship between the conditions in which the text is produced and the text itself. He is anxious to dispel the idea that

Charlotte Brontë was divorced from any kind of political, social, economic or cultural context, and argues instead that her novels are the result of combinations of events and movements that were taking place in the world around her. Haworth, he suggests, far from being a remote, untouched location, was in fact 'close to the centre of the West Riding woollen area ... [and] had several worsted mills and more than a century-old industry' nearby (ibid., p. 3). During Charlotte's lifetime, the West Riding was also the site of acute political tensions between the old land-owning classes and the new industrialists, and between the workers and the owners. On a more personal level, Charlotte felt herself in an **ambiguous** position to both industrialists and land-owners. As a clergyman's daughter, she had a certain status that made her the social equal of the gentry. But in economic terms, she had equality with neither factory-owners nor squires. She had also been brought up by a Calvinistic and conservative father to ideals of duty and submission, and to an unquestioning acceptance of the status quo. There is little doubt that she felt at odds with her upbringing and wanted to assert her opposition to a social world in which she effectively had no place. The consequence, Eagleton suggests, is that Charlotte's work is riven by:

> a constant struggle between two ambiguous, internally divided sets of values. On the one hand are ranged the values of rationality, coolness, shrewd self-seeking, energetic individualism, radical protest and rebellion; on the other hand lie the habits of piety, submission, culture, tradition, conservatism. (Ibid., p. 4)

Ambiguity was structural both to Charlotte's social situation and to her personality. She lived between the old values and emerging new ones. Thus, while it is certainly true that *Villette* is not a novel that deals explicitly with social problems such as industrialisation and urbanisation, those ideas are projected symbolically into Lucy's personal struggles. Eagleton argues that the 'fundamental structure of Charlotte's novels is a triadic one ... determined by a complex play between protagonist, a Romantic-radical and an autocratic conservative' (ibid., p. 74). In *Villette*, Lucy is the protagonist, M. Paul is the 'Romantic-radical' and the autocratic conservative is Madame Beck. Lucy's struggle is about where her own duty and self-interest should lie – duty and self-interest, of course, being oppositions. The figures in the triad are **analogous** with the matrices of current social debates: the reformer versus the conservative, with the protagonist agonisingly caught between them. In other words, Charlotte Brontë did not write explicitly about social issues in her fiction, but they are there in disguised and symbolic forms. Eagleton concludes that she resolved the conflicts in novels such as *Villette* through the 'mythical unity' of love (ibid., p. 75), which he argues is an evasion of the real problems and a retreat into fantasy. Such novels, he says, are **ideological** and finally unsatisfactory as confrontations with a complex reality. 'If it is a function of ideology to achieve an illusory resolution of real contradictions,' he writes, 'then Charlotte Brontë's novels are ideological in a precise sense – myths.' They are part of 'the complex mythology which constitutes Victorian bourgeois consciousness' (ibid., p. 97). In the end, *Villette* is a political cop-out.

PSYCHOANALYTIC APPROACHES

Psychoanalytic approaches to literature seek **repressed** traumas in the texts they study. Sigmund Freud argued that the process of reaching maturity involves giving up excess and unsuitable desires – for food, sex, attention. These desires, however, do not go away – they are repressed in the unconscious mind from where they occasionally mount escape bids. Freud called these escapes 'the return of the repressed' and suggested that they could be seen in any unwilled act, such as dreams, slips of the tongue, or repeated physical tics. Early psychoanalytical criticism focused its attention on the biography of the author, seeking psychosexual symptoms in his or her life and reading those symptoms into the texts s/he had produced. Later critics looked more carefully at character for such symptoms. The overwhelming focus of psychoanalytic criticism today is on the symptoms revealed by the text itself and their relationship to what might be thought of as the unconscious of a whole culture rather than the individual writer.

There is a long-standing presumption that literary texts are 'finished', complete works of art, which should, therefore, be consistent and coherent. When they do not conform to this notion, they are often judged as failing. A novel such as *Villette*, however, troubles the categories of completeness and coherence by often being internally contradictory. The critic Mary Jacobus, in an important essay entitled 'The Buried Letter: *Villette*' (in *Reading Woman: Essays in Feminist Criticism*, 1986), reads the contradictions of the novel as symptoms of repression, but instead of seeing the novel as somehow 'failing' or 'unhealthy', she argues that the repressive tendency is part of its artfulness. Starting with the moment when Lucy writes two different letters for Dr John ('one "under the dry stinting check of Reason", the other "according to the full, liberal impulse of Feeling" – one for his benefit … the other for hers' [ibid., p. 41]), Jacobus argues that *Villette* points two different ways: towards the conventions of **realism** and towards the incompatible conventions of **Romanticism**. Realism depends on rationalism and common sense, but although *Villette* draws on realist conventions, it is also a novel 'haunted' by dark secrets, Jesuit plots and ghostly nuns, features that have no place in the realist world. By **juxtaposing** two incongruous versions of the world, Jacobus argues, Brontë's text calls into question the common-sense view that the real is somehow the healthy, and the version of reality to which everyone should subscribe, whatever the personal cost. For Lucy the cost would be too great.

Jacobus's reading is especially interesting in its analysis of two textual features: the recurrent appearances and interpretation of the nun, and Lucy's view of the actress Vashti. On the one hand, there is clearly a realist explanation of the nun – Alfred de Hamal in a habit. On the other, the nun appears to Lucy only at moments of stress or emotional excitement – when she wants to be alone to read Dr John's letter (Chapter 22), when she resolves to bury John's letters (Chapter 26), and when her love for M. Paul first begins to receive real encouragement and both of them see a very substantial nun whose presence shakes the branches of a tree (Chapter 31). In other words, despite the nun's reality, s/he also appears to have a supernatural knowledge of when Lucy is experiencing forbidden desire. In the text there is an unconscious connection between haunting and love.

For Jacobus, too, Vashti is 'an aspect of [Lucy's] hidden revolt' (op. cit., p. 45). In other words, Lucy's tumultuous feelings are projected on to the actress, who is a 'satanic rebel and fallen angel' (ibid., p. 46). *Villette,* says Jacobus, 'can only be silent about the true nature of Lucy's oppression' – her condition as an unmarried, displaced woman in a culture that affords her no scope for her own desires. When Lucy describes Vashti, she indirectly describes her own feelings: 'what the novel cannot say is eloquently inscribed in its subtext – in the "discursive" activity of Lucy's (over-)heated imagination, and in the agitated notation and heightened language which signal it'. The necessity for repression (no matter how painful) is signalled 'with the fire that flames out during Vashti's performance' (ibid., p. 59), as well as by Dr John's disgust at the spectacle; to be that excitable, so desiring, is downright dangerous, leading to social judgement figured as death by fire.

Jacobus's conclusion is that *Villette* represses its own **feminist** message because of anxiety about where that message might lead. But she also argues that repression is not so much a symptom of psychological disorder in the novel as its very subject matter. *Villette*'s contradictions have to be understood not as artistic flaws but as a kind of adventure in psychological (as opposed to social) realism. But here psychology is more than an aspect of the individual: psychoanalysis has to approach whole societies as well as given individuals within them.

FEMINIST APPROACHES

Feminist criticism of literary texts has traditionally been concerned with three broad issues: the representation of women in literature (or images of women criticism); the position of the woman writer (often known as a **gynocritical** approach); and the special ways in which women respond – in revisions of plot and language, for example – to models established by a largely male **canon** of literature.

Sandra M. Gilbert and Susan Gubar's study, *The Madwoman in the Attic: The Place of the Woman Writer in the Nineteenth-Century Literary Imagination* (1979), exemplifies all three of these issues in its considerations of a range of writing by women in the nineteenth century. The book begins from the premise that the traditional approach to literature validates masculine points of view over feminine ones. In the nineteenth century, Gilbert and Gubar argue, the woman writer was in a particularly difficult position. If she wrote critically about the restrictions on women in the cultural and critical status quo, she was deemed to be unfeminine (nice women should not complain) and her writing was attacked as bad art (the critical standard depended on acceptance of the status quo). These conditions – along with the facts that women generally had less access to education and professional status in this period – meant that women's protests against their own limited lives were often couched in disguised terms rather than as overt protest.

Gilbert and Gubar's chapter on Charlotte Brontë's *Villette* (Chapter 12, 'The Buried Life of Lucy Snowe'), begins from the assumption that many models of self-fulfilment found in the literature of **Romanticism** are essentially masculine. Taking two examples from male-authored poetry – Matthew Arnold's 'The Buried Life' and William Wordsworth's 'Lucy' poems – they suggest that Lucy Snowe's story is a rewriting of the assumptions made by the male poets. Arnold's poem suggests that by meeting his beloved's eyes, he will see beneath the surface of conventional everyday life to the 'buried life' of sincere emotion and he will thereby be refreshed. Wordsworth's 'Lucy' poems are concerned with women who live 'hidden among untrodden ways ... [and function for the poet] as emblems for the calm and peace that nature brings' (ibid., p. 402). In both cases, the enforced privacy of female life is understood as the repository of virtue that will assuage the world-weary male poet's distress.

Lucy Snowe's name perhaps nods towards the 'Lucy' poems, Gilbert and Gubar suggest; but far from being calm and virtuous, her story articulates the tempestuousness that might lurk behind a calm surface. It is all very well for male poets who *choose* privacy (because they have a choice), to make privacy an ideal, but more important for Charlotte Brontë is 'the destructive effect of the buried life on women who can neither escape by retreating into the self ... nor find a solution by dehumanizing the other into a spiritual object' (ibid., p. 403). They see Lucy's story as an important feminist rewriting of the masculine tradition of Romanticism. And Arnold's distressed recognition that the novel is full of 'hunger, rebellion and rage' is in part the hurt recognition that his own ideal has been assaulted by the ideal figure turning out to have needs, desires and passions of her own.

Lucy is not calm because she is a divided self, caught between the social requirement that she should behave as propriety dictates and the urgent promptings of her own desire. This desire, however, is often projected on to other characters in the novel, Gilbert and Gubar suggest. Thus, for example, little Polly at Bretton 'acts out all those impulses already repressed by Lucy, so that the two girls represent two sides of Lucy's divided self' (ibid., p. 404). Other female characters operate in similar ways. Miss Marchmont, for example, is a 'monitory image' (ibid., p. 405), a warning of what Lucy might become if she agrees to be similarly confined. Madame Beck is both a role model (she occupies the social space that Lucy aspires to) and a warning. Ginevra 'embodies Lucy's attraction to self-indulgence and freedom' (ibid., p. 409).

Telling the story of achieving selfhood from a woman's point of view, suggest Gilbert and Gubar, is what gives *Villette* its structure. The novel is Brontë's 'attempt to create an adequate fiction of her own' rather than fitting her life into the ready-made models of fictional femininity. They read the creation of her own female characters and her re-creation of femininity in the different arts (the paintings in the gallery, the actress Vashti) as subversive re-readings of simplistic masculine versions of women. Vashti in particular is a forceful figure. In the biblical story from which her name is taken, Vashti is commanded by her husband to display her beauty before the court, but she 'refuses to be treated as an object' (ibid., p. 424). Her symbolic significance in the novel comes from the fact that her denial of male authority is subversive (and even 'inflammatory' since the theatre is literally set alight by it); but the personal cost is enormous – Vashti is both consumed by her own talent and rejected by the society she criticises. The novel expresses the pain of Lucy's situation in Vashti's remarkable acting. But it remains finally an uncomfortable novel because it can offer no solution to the problems its identifies.

FURTHER READING

BIOGRAPHY

Edward Chitham and Tom Winnifrith, *Charlotte and Emily Brontë*, Macmillan, London, 1989

Juliet Gardiner, *The World Within: The Brontës at Haworth: A Life in Letters, Diaries and Writings*, Collins and Brown, London, 1992

Elizabeth Gaskell, *The Life of Charlotte Brontë* (1857), Penguin Books, Harmondsworth, 1975

Winifred Gérin, *Charlotte Brontë: The Evolution of Genius*, Oxford University Press, Oxford, 1971

Lyndall Gordon, *Charlotte Brontë: A Passionate Life*, Vintage, London, 1995

HISTORICAL AND LITERARY BACKGROUND

Nancy Armstrong, *Desire and Domestic Fiction: A Political History of the Novel*, Oxford University Press, Oxford, 1989

Frances Power Cobbe, 'What shall we do with our old maids?', *Frazer's Magazine*, November 1862, reprinted in Susan Hamilton (ed.), *Criminals, Idiots, Women and Minors: Victorian Writing by Women on Women*, Broadview Press, Ontario, 1996

George Eliot, 'Silly Novels by Lady Novelists', *Westminster Review*, October 1856, in *Selected Essays, Poems and Other Writings*, A.S. Byatt (ed.), Penguin Books, Harmondsworth, 1990

Elizabeth Deeds Ermath, *The English Novel in History: 1840–1895*, Routledge, London, 1997

Harriet Devine Jump (ed.), *Women's Writing of the Victorian Period, an Anthology 1837–1901*, Edinburgh University Press, Edinburgh, 1999

Sigmund Freud, 'The Uncanny' (1919) in *The Penguin Freud Library*, Volume 14, *Art and Literature*, Albert Dickson (ed.), Penguin Books, Harmondsworth, 1990

Mary Poovey, *Uneven Developments: The Ideological Work of Gender in Mid-Nineteenth-Century England*, Virago, London, 1989

Elaine Showalter, *A Literature of Their Own: Women Novelists from Brontë to Lessing*, 2nd edition, Virago, London, 1982

Raymond Williams, *The English Novel from Dickens to Lawrence*, Hogarth Press, London, 1985

CRITICAL STUDIES OF CHARLOTTE BRONTË

Miriam Allott (ed.), *Charlotte Brontë: Jane Eyre and Villette: A Selection of Critical Essays*, Casebook Series, Macmillan, London, 1973

Penny Boumelha, *Charlotte Brontë: Key Women Writers*, Indiana University Press, Bloomington and Indianopolis, 1990

Terry Eagleton, *Myths of Power: A Marxist Study of the Brontës*, 2nd edition, Macmillan, London, 1988

Sandra M. Gilbert and Susan Gubar, *The Madwoman in the Attic: The Place of the Woman Writer in the Nineteenth-Century Literary Imagination*, Yale University Press, Yale, 1979

Mary Jacobus, *Reading Woman: Essays in Feminist Criticism*, Columbia University Press, New York, 1986

John Kucich, *Repression in Victorian Fiction: Charlotte Brontë, George Eliot and Charles Dickens*, University of California Press, Los Angeles and Berkeley, 1987

Pauline Nestor (ed.), *Villette: Contemporary Critical Essays*, New Casebook Series, Macmillan, Basingstoke, 1992

History	Charlotte's life	Literature
1811 First Luddite riot, Nottingham		
	1812 Patrick Brontë, an Irish Protestant clergyman, marries Maria Branwell, a Cornish Methodist from Penzance	
1813-17 Luddites executed, York. Movement broken	**1813** Birth of Maria **1813-18** Patrick Brontë publishes a collection of poems and two novels	**1813** Jane Austen, *Pride and Prejudice*
1815 Napoleon escapes from Elba, becomes emperor and is defeated at Waterloo	**1815** Birth of Elizabeth	**1815** Byron, *Completed Works*
	1816 Birth of Charlotte	**1816** Jane Austen, *Emma*
	1817 Birth of Branwell	**1817** Death of Jane Austen
	1818 Birth of Emily **1819** The Brontë family move to Haworth in Yorkshire	**1818** Mary Shelley, *Frankenstein*
1820 Death of George III (end of Regency), and accession of George IV, who attempts to dissolve his marriage to Caroline. Death of Napoleon	**1820** Birth of Anne	
	1821 Mrs Maria Brontë dies of cancer, and her sister, Elizabeth Branwell, comes to care for the children	**1821** Death of poet John Keats
		1824 Death of poet Lord Byron
1825 First railway opened between Stockton and Darlington	**1825** Both Maria and Elizabeth die of tuberculosis at Cowan Bridge School	
1829 Catholic emancipation in Britain		
1830 Death of George IV and accession of William IV		

History	Charlotte's life	Literature

1830s Abolitionists of Slave Trade active in America; articles in *Monthly Repository* by W.J. Fox and W.B. Adams influenced by Harriet Taylor

1831 Cholera epidemic

1831 Charlotte boards at Roe Head School, Mirfield

1832 First Reform Act

1832 Death of Sir Walter Scott and Goethe; Harriet Martineau, *Illustrations of Political Economy;* Anna Jameson, *Characteristics of Women*

1833 Slavery abolished in the British Empire

1834 Establishment of Union Workhouses; Tolpuddle Martyrs

1835-8 Charlotte returns to Roe Head as a teacher, with Emily as a pupil, but after three months of homesickness, Emily returns to Haworth

1836 Charles Dickens, *The Pickwick Papers*

1837 Death of William IV; accession of Queen Victoria

1838 'People's Charter' published

1839 Chartist petition rejected by Parliament – riots in Birmingham

1839 Charlotte, now a governess, visits Norton Conyers, near Ripon, model for Thornfield Hall. Charlotte turns down two proposals of marriage: from her friend Ellen Nussey's clergyman brother, and from an Irish clergyman

1840 Penny Post established

1840 Death of novelist Fanny Burney

1841 Charlotte becomes governess to a family near Bradford

1842 Second Chartist petition presented and rejected

1842 Charlotte and Emily study French in Brussels at the Hegers' school

1843 Charlotte returns to Brussels to teach and falls in love with Monsieur Heger

1843 Margaret Fuller (American journalist), 'The Great Lawsuit – Man versus Men. Woman versus Women', *The Dial*

History	Charlotte's life	Literature
	1844 Charlotte returns home when her father becomes almost totally blind	
1845 Famine in Ireland due to potato blight		**1845** Margaret Fuller, *Women in the Nineteenth Century*
1846 Repeal of the Corn Laws	**1846** *Poems by Currer, Ellis and Acton Bell* are published by the three sisters	**1846** Margaret Fuller visits Britain
	1847 Charlotte's *Jane Eyre* is published under the pseudonym of Currer Bell; Anne's *Agnes Grey* is published under the pseudonym of Acton Bell; Emily's *Wuthering Heights* is published under the pseudonym of Ellis Bell	**1847** William Thackeray, *Vanity Fair* (serialisation)
1848 Final Chartist petition rejected. Revolutions in Paris, Berlin, Vienna, Venice, Rome, Milan, Naples, Prague and Budapest; Marx and Engel publish *Communist Manifesto*	**1848** Anne's *The Tenant of Wildfell Hall* is published; Branwell dies of alcoholism; Emily dies of tuberculosis	**1848** Elizabeth Gaskell, *Mary Barton*
1849 Cholera epidemic	**1849** Anne dies of tuberculosis; Charlotte, the only surviving sibling, publishes *Shirley*	**1849-54** *Eliza Cook's Journal*
	1849-51 Charlotte visits London and meets writers of her day: Mrs Gaskell, Harriet Martineau, William Thackeray	
1851 The Great Exhibition at the Crystal Palace		**1851** Harriet Taylor, 'Enfranchisement of Women', in *Westminster Review*
		1852 Harriet Beecher Stowe, *Uncle Tom's Cabin*
	1853 Charlotte publishes ***Villette***, based on her experiences in Brussels	
1854 Cholera epidemic	**1854** Charlotte marries her father's curate, Arthur Nicholls	
	1855 Charlotte is pregnant, but dies from a combination of ill health and pneumonia before reaching full term	

allusion a passing reference in a work of literature to a text beyond itself. A writer may allude to historical facts, legends, or to other literary works, or even to autobiographical details. Some kinds of literary allusion are related to parody, where they take place for comic effect. In *Villette*, however, allusion is primarily a method of achieving extended authority for Lucy's narrative, since the texts to which she habitually refers are the Bible and classic works of English literature

ambiguity the capacity of words and sentences, and, indeed, whole texts, to have uncertain or multiple meanings. A pun is the simplest form of ambiguity, where a single word with two sharply contrasted meanings is used, usually for comic effect. Ambiguity can arise also from syntax (where it is difficult to disentangle the grammar of a sentence to resolve the meaning), and from tone (where the reader cannot decide whether a given text is to be taken seriously or not); its effects can be unsettling rather than merely comic

analogy a parallel or comparison. A word, thing, idea or story, chosen for the purpose of comparison, which can be used to explain whatever it is compared with

autobiographical fiction a complex and contradictory term. Autobiography means the writing of one's own life, so an autobiographical fiction might be any novel written in the first person. Confusion can arise from the presumption that the first-person speaker in the novel is intimately connected with the actual author. This presumption is supported in *Villette* by the fact that Charlotte Brontë used parts of her own experience in the novel. However, the reader must not confuse Brontë's biography with Lucy's – they are not the same person

Bildungsroman a novel that describes a protagonist's development from childhood to maturity. Like autobiography, *Bildungsroman* tends to focus on the relationships between experience, education, character and identity. Unlike autobiography, *Bildungsroman* need not be written in the first person

canon originally applied to those books of the Bible that had been accepted by Church authorities as containing the word of God. More recently, in literary studies, it has come to mean the 'great books' or 'great tradition' of texts that everyone should know in order to be considered educated in literature. The means by which the canon has been constructed, however, have been exclusionary – leaving out, for example, works written by those in marginal or excluded groups (women, the working classes, non-white authors and homosexual writers) – so the concept of the canon has come in for much recent scrutiny as a result

cliché a phrase, situation or type of character made dull by overuse

denouement the resolution of the plot, when all the strands reach their conclusion

disjunction mismatch between tone and content or between appearance and reality

fantasy playful imagining; the term usually describes literature that deals with imaginary worlds divorced from reality, but it can also mean a dream that is unlikely but not impossible

femininity literary critics and sociologists distinguish between the biological sex of a given subject (male or female) and the social or cultural attributes associated with them (masculinity or femininity). In the mid-Victorian period, femininity meant passivity, docility, domesticity and general weakness, attributes that do not necessarily or naturally belong to women, but which were culturally and socially sanctioned by the norms of the period

feminist criticism this term covers a large variety of approaches to literature. All the approaches, however, share an interest in women – as characters, readers and writers. Feminist criticism is politically motivated, seeking to analyse and understand the reasons for female inequality in the past and today

foreshadow to suggest in advance what will happen later

genre a type or kind of literature. The three major divisions of writing are poetry, drama and prose, which may be further subdivided. A novel, for example, might be a romance, a thriller or a fantasy. The importance of genre is that it gives readers a horizon of expectation, a set of criteria against which to judge the piece before them. For example, an unfunny comedy fails to meet its audience's expectations of the genre

Gothic the word 'Gothic' originally referred to a German tribe, but it came also to be associated with medieval art and architecture. Gothic fiction, which has traditionally been set in medieval buildings such as castles or convents, tended from the eighteenth century onwards to deal in cruel passions and supernatural terrors. It has also come to mean any work of fiction that deals with obsessive, gloomy or frightening feelings – whether or not they are supernatural, and whether or not they have a medieval setting. In the nineteenth and twentieth centuries, 'Gothic' has been used to describe fictions based on abnormal psychological states

gynocritical 'woman-centred' approaches in feminist literary theories; these writings concentrate on female writers, readers and characters in their analysis

ideology the collection of ideas, opinions, values, beliefs and preconceptions that go to make up the mind-set of a group of people, that is, the intellectual framework through which they view everything, and which colours all their attitudes and feelings (especially, perhaps, assumptions about power and authority). What we take to be reality is controlled by the ideologies of the era in which we live. In literary theory, ideology means the unconscious motivations behind a writer and his/her text – the beliefs that the writer holds without analysing them. In *Villette*, for example, Lucy believes that love is a good thing that will rescue her from her lonely life. Charlotte Brontë does not analyse this belief, but takes it for granted, and, as such, it is an ideological motivation that lies behind the novel

irony consists of saying one thing and meaning another. It is achieved by understatement, overstatement, concealment or allusion rather than by direct statement

juxtapose to place close together for contrast

literalisation making metaphors come true. Since many metaphors have become almost clichés, writers can get striking effects by literalization. In *Villette*, Lucy describes how she knocks her desires on the head (represses them) by the literal image of Jael knocking Sisera on the head with a hammer and nail

masquerade originally a masked ball or street carnival in which the participants wore disguise. More recently, the term has been used to describe the ways in which gender roles are learned and performed: masculinity and femininity are not the natural attributes of men and women so much as the performance – the mask – they put on in order to pass muster in the world

metaphor an implied comparison, e.g. She sailed into the room; this does not directly compare two things, but suggests a likeness (here, between a woman and a ship) without using the words 'like' or 'as'

parody an imitation of a specific work of literature (in prose or verse) in a style devised to ridicule its characteristic features. More broadly, parody can also mean any kind of playful imitation: in *Villette* Graham parodies adult behaviour in his first conversations with Polly

periphrasis an indirect manner of speech, sometimes used for comic purposes, sometimes used to disguise unpleasantness

psychoanalytic criticism drawing on the texts of clinical psychoanalysts such as Sigmund Freud, Carl Gustav Jung and Jacques Lacan, psychoanalytic criticism analyses literature according to theories of the mind. It seeks the unconscious motivations of the text rather than the story it explicitly seeks to tell, looking for instances of repression and symptoms of it returning to the conscious mind in the surface of the writing

realism a tendency in literature to portray the real world without softening its appearance (as idealist or romantic fictions do); realism aims to tell the unglossed truth. It refers to a set of conventions by which the real might be expressed, not to reality itself – realist literature is not *real*, but is attempting to reflect reality. It was the dominant mode of nineteenth-century fiction, but the term is often misleading because of the constraints on what could be represented to a conservative Victorian readership. The reality that realism portrayed was frankly very selective

repression in psychoanalytical thought, repression is the process by which forbidden thoughts and desires are placed in the unconscious. They return to the conscious mind through unwilled symptoms, such as dreams, slips of the tongue, physical tics and other neurotic signs

romance, romantic fiction romance originally referred to medieval fictions that dealt with adventures in chivalry and love. In more recent usage, romantic fiction describes any prose work whose primary interest is in love. Such fictions tend to have certain stock features, including a beautiful heroine and her handsome lover

Romanticism not to be confused with romance, Romanticism is a term usually used to describe a movement in literature from around 1780 to 1830. Romantic writing is more concerned with emotion than form and is often associated with extreme forms of individualism, irrationality and supernaturalism, political radicalism and revolution, the love of nature, formal innovation in poetry, and dismissive attitudes to the conservative positions of decorum, propriety, order and rationality

separate spheres debate from the mid-nineteenth century onwards there was a series of debates in the British press about the proper relationships between men and women. This Victorian 'battle of the sexes' came to be known as the separate spheres debate because of the argument then current among contemporary conservative writers that a woman's sphere was the home, and a man's was the public domain. Many Victorian writers believed that a woman's role was entirely bound up with domesticity, with being a good wife and mother; a man's role was to support her by performing his public duties in the world of paid work. The debate became more polarised as the century progressed, since it was becoming very clear that many women could not marry (there were not enough men in the population), so they too would have to seek properly remunerated work outside the home, thereby breaking out of the domestic sphere

stereotype a fixed idea or a standard mental impression. It is often used to describe a clichéd figure, or a stock character in certain types of drama or fiction

stock character recognisable type of character associated with a particular genre. In a comedy of manners, for example, stock characters include the rake, the *ingénue* (or innocent) and the older female battle-axe. Stock characters are stereotypes

uncanny literally 'unknown'. This term is used to describe strange and weird events, such as an inanimate object taking on human characteristics. Although readers may be aware that such visions spring from dreams, delusions or mistakes, they also know that they are real to the character(s) experiencing them. For this reason, the uncanny is a psychological effect, being a product of the human mind. Freud's word for the uncanny is *unheimlich*, literally 'unhomely' – a good description of weird experiences that (more often than not) occur outside the home in unfamiliar surroundings

voyeurism an unhealthy obsession with looking; a spying that produces a quasi-sexual satisfaction in the viewer

Ruth Robbins is Senior Lecturer in English at University College, Northampton. She is the author of *Literary Feminisms* and co-editor with Julian Wolfreys of *Victorian Gothic*. She has published many articles on Victorian literature and on literary theory, as well as writing York Notes on Oscar Wilde's *The Importance of Being Earnest* and Angela Carter's *Nights at the Circus*.

York Notes Advanced (£3.99 each)

Margaret Atwood
Cat's Eye

Margaret Atwood
The Handmaid's Tale

Jane Austen
Mansfield Park

Jane Austen
Persuasion

Jane Austen
Pride and Prejudice

Jane Austen
Sense and Sensibility

Alan Bennett
Talking Heads

William Blake
Songs of Innocence and of Experience

Charlotte Brontë
Jane Eyre

Charlotte Brontë
Villette

Emily Brontë
Wuthering Heights

Angela Carter
Nights at the Circus

Geoffrey Chaucer
The Franklin's Prologue and Tale

Geoffrey Chaucer
The Miller's Prologue and Tale

Geoffrey Chaucer
Prologue To the Canterbury Tales

Geoffrey Chaucer
The Wife of Bath's Prologue and Tale

Samuel Taylor Coleridge
Selected Poems

Joseph Conrad
Heart of Darkness

Daniel Defoe
Moll Flanders

Charles Dickens
Great Expectations

Charles Dickens
Hard Times

Emily Dickinson
Selected Poems

John Donne
Selected Poems

Carol Ann Duffy
Selected Poems

George Eliot
Middlemarch

George Eliot
The Mill on the Floss

T.S. Eliot
Selected Poems

F. Scott Fitzgerald
The Great Gatsby

E.M. Forster
A Passage to India

Brian Friel
Translations

Thomas Hardy
Jude the Obscure

Thomas Hardy
The Mayor of Casterbridge

Thomas Hardy
The Return of the Native

Thomas Hardy
Selected Poems

Thomas Hardy
Tess of the d'Urbervilles

Seamus Heaney
Selected Poems from Opened Ground

Nathaniel Hawthorne
The Scarlet Letter

Homer
The Odyssey

Kazuo Ishiguro
The Remains of the Day

Ben Jonson
The Alchemist

James Joyce
Dubliners

John Keats
Selected Poems

Christopher Marlowe
Doctor Faustus

Arthur Miller
Death of a Salesman

John Milton
Paradise Lost Books I & II

Toni Morrison
Beloved

Sylvia Plath
Selected Poems

Alexander Pope
Rape of the Lock and other poems

William Shakespeare
Antony and Cleopatra

William Shakespeare
As You Like It

William Shakespeare
Hamlet

William Shakespeare
King Lear

William Shakespeare
Macbeth

William Shakespeare
Measure for Measure

William Shakespeare
The Merchant of Venice

William Shakespeare
A Midsummer Night's Dream

William Shakespeare
Much Ado About Nothing

William Shakespeare
Othello

William Shakespeare
Richard II

William Shakespeare
Romeo and Juliet

William Shakespeare
The Taming of the Shrew

William Shakespeare
The Tempest

William Shakespeare
Twelfth Night

William Shakespeare
The Winter's Tale

George Bernard Shaw
Saint Joan

Mary Shelley
Frankenstein

Jonathan Swift
Gulliver's Travels and A Modest Proposal

Alfred, Lord Tennyson
Selected Poems

Alice Walker
The Color Purple

Oscar Wilde
The Importance of Being Earnest

Tennessee Williams
A Streetcar Named Desire

John Webster
The Duchess of Malfi

Virginia Woolf
To the Lighthouse

W.B. Yeats
Selected Poems

Jane Austen
Emma

Louis de Bernières
Captain Corelli's Mandolin

Caryl Churchill
Top Girls and *Cloud Nine*

Charles Dickens
Bleak House

T.S. Eliot
The Waste Land

Homer
The Iliad

Aldous Huxley
Brave New World

Christopher Marlowe
Edward II

George Orwell
Nineteen Eighty-four

William Shakespeare
Henry IV Pt I

William Shakespeare
Henry IV Part II

William Shakespeare
Richard III

Tom Stoppard
Arcadia and *Rosencrantz and Guildenstern are Dead*

Virgil
The Aeneid

Jeanette Winterson
Oranges are Not the Only Fruit

Tennessee Williams
Cat on a Hot Tin Roof

Metaphysical Poets

GCSE and equivalent levels (£3.50 each)

Maya Angelou
I Know Why the Caged Bird Sings

Jane Austen
Pride and Prejudice

Alan Ayckbourn
Absent Friends

Elizabeth Barrett Browning
Selected Poems

Robert Bolt
A Man for All Seasons

Harold Brighouse
Hobson's Choice

Charlotte Brontë
Jane Eyre

Emily Brontë
Wuthering Heights

Shelagh Delaney
A Taste of Honey

Charles Dickens
David Copperfield

Charles Dickens
Great Expectations

Charles Dickens
Hard Times

Charles Dickens
Oliver Twist

Roddy Doyle
Paddy Clarke Ha Ha Ha

George Eliot
Silas Marner

George Eliot
The Mill on the Floss

Anne Frank
The Diary of Anne Frank

William Golding
Lord of the Flies

Oliver Goldsmith
She Stoops To Conquer

Willis Hall
The Long and the Short and the Tall

Thomas Hardy
Far from the Madding Crowd

Thomas Hardy
The Mayor of Casterbridge

Thomas Hardy
Tess of the d'Urbervilles

Thomas Hardy
The Withered Arm and other Wessex Tales

L.P. Hartley
The Go-Between

Seamus Heaney
Selected Poems

Susan Hill
I'm the King of the Castle

Barry Hines
A Kestrel for a Knave

Louise Lawrence
Children of the Dust

Harper Lee
To Kill a Mockingbird

Laurie Lee
Cider with Rosie

Arthur Miller
The Crucible

Arthur Miller
A View from the Bridge

Robert O'Brien
Z for Zachariah

Frank O'Connor
My Oedipus Complex and Other Stories

George Orwell
Animal Farm

J.B. Priestley
An Inspector Calls

J.B. Priestley
When We Are Married

Willy Russell
Educating Rita

Willy Russell
Our Day Out

J.D. Salinger
The Catcher in the Rye

William Shakespeare
Henry IV Part 1

William Shakespeare
Henry V

William Shakespeare
Julius Caesar

William Shakespeare
Macbeth

William Shakespeare
The Merchant of Venice

William Shakespeare
A Midsummer Night's Dream

William Shakespeare
Much Ado About Nothing

William Shakespeare
Romeo and Juliet

William Shakespeare
The Tempest

William Shakespeare
Twelfth Night

George Bernard Shaw
Pygmalion

Mary Shelley
Frankenstein

R.C. Sherriff
Journey's End

Rukshana Smith
Salt on the Snow

John Steinbeck
Of Mice and Men

Robert Louis Stevenson
Dr Jekyll and Mr Hyde

Jonathan Swift
Gulliver's Travels

Robert Swindells
Daz 4 Zoe

Mildred D. Taylor
Roll of Thunder, Hear My Cry

Mark Twain
Huckleberry Finn

James Watson
Talking in Whispers

Edith Wharton
Ethan Frome

William Wordsworth
Selected Poems

A Choice of Poets

Mystery Stories of the Nineteenth Century including The Signalman

Nineteenth Century Short Stories

Poetry of the First World War

Six Women Poets